I0438919

TABLE OF CONTENTS

INTRODUCTION

The term counterterrorism, largely absent from popular use in the United States (U.S.) prior to the 1990s, emerged as dominant part of U.S. vocabulary and thought in the post-Cold War era. The terrorist attack of September 11, 2001 (September 11th) became the watershed moment that infused the concept of terrorism, and consequently counterterrorism, into the American psyche, but this attack did not signify the first international terrorist threat against the U.S. homeland. Though September 11th combined surprise with devastation, the U.S. government began efforts to combat terrorism on U.S. soil long before that fateful fall day.

The first World Trade Center attack in 1993, the Oklahoma City bombing in 1995, and the 1996 Olympics bombing shaped U.S. domestic counterterrorism efforts in the 1990s. The most significant acts of terrorism in the United States prior to September 11th signaled two things to the American public. First, the start of the post-Cold War era did not necessarily mean the United States was invulnerable. Next, the successful disruption of plots leading up to the millennium and the prosecution of terrorists in federal court meant the existing system could handle the new threat. In part, success bred a new false sense of security because the federal government had defeated terrorism's symptoms, but not its root causes. Agencies cooperated, shared information, and reached narrow goals centered on a few focused criminal investigations. There was no catalyst to induce sweeping change to the system, so ad hoc adjustments were the order of the day.

Until September 11th, the United States lacked significant reason to revolutionize its existing counterterrorism paradigm as would be seen in its aftermath. Reacting to the catastrophe rapidly to rally a frightened public and dissuade future aggressors, the federal government developed a counterterrorism strategy without the benefit of time for detailed analysis. Leaders in Washington succeeded in stabilizing the nation, recognizing a new threat, and preventing another attack. Crucially, with new perspective on the threat of violent extremism, the government pushed for a new counterterrorism paradigm. Judging the success of these reforms is central to further strengthening the United States against the terrorists of tomorrow.

More than ten years after the United States commenced a campaign against terrorism, many questions linger about not only the nature of the threat, but also the nation's strategic response. The creation the Department of Homeland Security (DHS), prolonged overseas military engagements, and legislation increasing powers for law enforcement and intelligence personnel demonstrate the widespread effects of September 11th. These responses have created a new meaning for a Whole-of-Government answer to extremism, but not without limitations. Existing policy has struggled to exploit central players in the domestic counterterrorism arena: state and local law enforcement.

Although the nation has avoided an attack on the scale of September 11th, serious questions remain about U.S. counterterrorism as it pertains to protecting the homeland. The changes that followed those attacks shaped a decade of counterterrorism policy, but persisting plots and continued criticisms of DHS necessitate a closer examination of current strategy. Reviewing the strengths and weaknesses in counterterrorism policy, and applying them to better planning is necessary to forge a more comprehensive and lasting strategy. With the exception of the current economic downturn, few other issues wield the potential to unite the diverse and powerful instruments of the interagency community, so the opportunity for substantive reform exists. Additionally, decreasing U.S. military engagement in Iraq and Afghanistan signals a new shift in overall U.S. counterterrorism posture. Most agree that more can be done, but divisions exist among which course provides the most security for the United States.

Thesis Statement

Improved interagency coordination combined with more equal partnerships with state and local law enforcement that exploit local capacity will strengthen U.S. domestic counterterrorism efforts.

Methodology

Assessing current U.S. counterterrorism policy, identifying positive and negative trends, and recommending adjustments is a complex undertaking. Examining the various parts of the counterterrorism machine individually as well as a collective is necessary to understand this dynamic environment. The analysis begins generally before delving into specific case studies to elucidate tangible examples that will shape this paper's recommendations.

Chapter 1 identifies key vocabulary and definitions needed to understand the arguments made in this paper. Next, Chapter 2 explores the Federal Bureau of Investigation's (FBI) central role in U.S. counterterrorism. As the lead agency for responding to domestic terrorism, any discussion of the subject naturally begins here. Exploring the FBI's legacy and role in the spotlight demonstrates its evolving approach to counterterrorism. In Chapter 3, the discussion switches to the other driving forces of U.S. policy: the National Security Council, Homeland Security Council, DHS, the Office of the Director of National Intelligence and its subordinate National Counterterrorism Center. The interplay between these actors is a microcosm for the wider interagency

3

counterterrorism community, characterized by diverging interests among a sprawling bureaucratic process.

Next, this paper employs three case studies to illustrate competing developments in counterterrorism and homeland security policy in the decade since September 11th. Reviewing the details of various responses to terrorism to include motivations behind these initiatives, notable successes or failures, and the applicability of these programs to communities large and small refines the focus of this effort to a manageable task. A first case study reviews the top-down federal response as exemplified by the creation of DHS in Chapter 4. It examines Washington's reliance on grant programs and questions the results of ten years of funding localities across the country. Similarly, it discusses the DHS role supporting the growth of fusion centers since 2001 while assessing the value of this initiative.

Chapter 5 reverses the angle, examining the bottom-up approach through a case study of the New York City Police Department, which forged its own counterterrorism agenda despite the concerns of its federal associates. A final case study comes in Chapter 6's appraisal of a potential middle ground, the Joint Terrorism Task Force (JTTF) model. Growing exponentially since 2001, the JTTF has been widely praised as an efficient and collaborative partnership between the federal government and state and local law enforcement. Exploring this model's ability to empower state and local actors and present wider lessons for the counterterrorism debate, this chapter judges the "jointness" of the JTTF.

The final section of this paper filters the three case studies through the prism of two enduring themes: interagency coordination and more equal partnerships. Using concrete examples of both missteps and victories in the last decade, it draws recommendations for moving towards true federal leadership, but not dominance, in the expansive counterterrorism enterprise while buttressing the need for a partnership with state and local actors that goes beyond the status quo. Following the introduction of several key recommendations, attention turns to overall conclusions from this effort.

CHAPTER 1: DEFINING TERRORISM AND COUNTERTERRORISM

Introducing Key Phrases

This chapter examines the origins of the several key terms, most notably terrorism and counterterrorism according to the U.S. government perspective. Since numerous U.S. organizations employ slightly different definitions, this chapter briefly introduces competing perspectives on those essential terms. After exploring the development of these words and their impact on government efforts to protect the United States, this chapter presents accepted definitions that will simplify further thesis investigation.

What Is Terrorism?

Understanding counterterrorism policy is incumbent on understanding what terrorism means to the U.S. government. Different individuals and agencies use different words that add to the challenges in executing an integrated national policy, so a basic understanding of what terrorism means for the United States is a good starting point for this discussion.

Dating back to 1969, the U.S. Code of Federal Regulations said "[t]errorism includes the unlawful use of force and violence against persons or property to intimidate or coerce a government, the civilian population, or any segment thereof, in furtherance of political or social objectives."[1] Additionally, Title 18 of U.S. Code goes another step and differentiates between domestic terrorism and international terrorism; consequently, the former applies to acts committed inside the United States by domestically-based actors

---

[1] Code of Federal Regulations, *Title 28 §0.85: Judicial Administration*, Government Printing Office (Washington, DC, 1969).

while the latter refers to acts both inside and outside the United States.[2] The distinction is important because it judges the bombing of the Oklahoma City Federal Building as domestic terrorism while the 9/11 Attacks on U.S. soil and the 1998 Africa Embassy Attacks are both classified as international terrorism. The Congressional Research Service notes that "[s]ome consider all terrorist plots occurring within the homeland as acts of domestic terrorism," but goes on to highlight that other federal sources prove this definition to be too broad.[3]

While various U.S. government sources use different definitions for historical, legal, or other reasons, finding a common terminology avoids misinterpretation and provides a better foundation for interagency efforts against terrorism. This paper accepts the enduring definition of terrorism from the 1969 Code of Federal Regulations listed above that the Federal Bureau of Investigation as the lead federal agency for countering terrorism continues to employ.[4]

Counterterrorism, Combating Terrorism & Anti-Terrorism

The broad spectrum of actions designed to neutralize terrorism are sometimes called counterterrorism, combating terrorism, or anti-terrorism. Each of these holds different meanings, so it is important to parse these terms early. The U.S. Department of Defense defines anti-terrorism as, "Defensive measures used to reduce the vulnerability of individuals and property to terrorist acts, to include rapid containment by local military

---

[2] Code of Federal Regulations, *Title 18 §2331:Crimes and Criminal Procedure*, Government Printing Office (Washington, DC, 1988).

[3] Congressional Research Service, *The Domestic Terrorist Threat: Background and Issues for Congress, by Jerome P. Bjelopera, Specialist in Organized Crime and Terrorism, Congressional Research Service, May 15, 2012* (Washington, DC: Government Printing Office, 2012), 2.

[4] Ibid., 3.

and civilian forces."[5] Of the three terms, anti-terrorism is the most narrow and tactical, so it does not figure prominently in this paper. Alternately, counterterrorism is defined as "Actions taken directly against terrorist networks and indirectly to influence and render global and regional environments inhospitable to terrorist networks."[6] Anti-terrorism connotes a defensive response to the symptoms of terrorism while counterterrorism includes offensive actions against terrorism's root causes.

Combating Terrorism was generally favored in the pre – 9/11 Era and includes "preventing and deterring terrorism; responding to a terrorist crisis, and managing the consequences after a terrorist attack."[7] Capturing not only prevention, but also response and resilience, the phrase combating terrorism gives greater specificity to counterterrorism, but ultimately remains subordinate to the wider counterterrorism term. Current U.S. policy supports employment of the term counterterrorism, as witnessed in the President's National Strategy for Counterterrorism released in 2011 and the founding of the National Counterterrorism Center at the behest of the 9/11 Commission.

For this paper's purposes, counterterrorism is the term of choice because it examines the entire spectrum of efforts to respond to terrorism. Since the focus of this paper is improving U.S. counterterrorism with respect to protecting the United States against attacks, it must also consider areas of overlap with the phrase homeland security. The term "homeland security" has faced persistent criticisms since its inception, but where a Department of Homeland Security is inextricably linked to many U.S.

---

[5] U.S. Joint Chiefs of Staff, *Joint Tactics, Techniques, and Procedures for Antiterrorism*, Joint Publication 3-07.2 (Washington DC: Joint Chiefs of Staff, March 17, 1998), I-1.
    [6] U.S. Joint Chiefs of Staff, *Counterterrorism*, Joint Publication 3-26 (Washington DC: Joint Chiefs of Staff, November 13, 2009), I-2.
    [7] General Accounting Office (GAO), *Combating Terrorism: Issues to Be Resolved to Improve Counterterrorism Operations, by the GAO, May 1999* (Washington, D.C: Government Printing Office, 1999).

counterterrorism functions, so too is its vocabulary. The 2010 Quadrennial Homeland Security Review notes that homeland security "describes the intersection of evolving threats and hazards with the traditional governmental and civic responsibilities of civil defense, emergency response, law enforcement, customs, border control, and immigration."[8] Efforts to improve U.S. domestic counterterrorism must include, but not be limited to, homeland security.

Supporting an All-Inclusive Approach

Examining the various definitions of counterterrorism also offers the reader an understanding of complexity of the U.S. government response. Though responding to terrorism unifies many government actors, differences in vocabulary hamper efforts to truly create a Whole-of-Government or even deeper, all-of-Nation approach, the final two important terms. The 2010 National Security Strategy released by President Barack Obama called for a Whole-of-Government approach that would, "update, balance, and integrate all of the tools of American power."[9] Expanding on that initiative, the White House released Presidential Policy Directive 8: National Preparedness, which called for a more inclusive all-of-Nation approach to consider instruments of power beyond simply the federal government.[10] Whereas the Whole-of-Government model sought to leverage the diverse body of government actors, the developing all-of-Nation model includes engaging not only state and local government partners, but also the American public and private enterprises too by leveraging their strengths against terrorism.

---

[8] U.S. Department of Homeland Security, *Quadrennial Homeland Security Review Report: A Strategic Framework for a Secure Homeland*, Government Printing Office (Washington, DC, 2010), 11.

[9] U.S. President, *National Security Strategy* (Washington, DC: Government Printing Office, May 2010), 14-16.

[10] U.S. President, *Presidential Policy Directive 8: National Preparedness* (Washington, DC: Government Printing Office, March 30, 2011), 1.

With these two approaches forming the foundation of current U.S. national security policy, a likely next step is to better leverage state and local governments, particularly law enforcement, in counterterrorism. Moving forward with an appreciation for the sometimes tenuous employment of these terms, but an appropriate understanding of them in the context of this paper will support the backbone of its thesis.

CHAPTER 2: THE FEDERAL BUREAU OF INVESTIGATION (FBI) LEAD FEDERAL AGENCY

The FBI: Historical Hegemon

In the history of American bureaucracy, the success of new institutions is largely relative to the standing of those institutions that came before. Since there is no pool of unclaimed powers that can be imbued upon a new player, these groups are born only through a diffusion of power from others within the existing system. Discussions of changes to U.S. counterterrorism posture rightly begin with the historical hegemon: the FBI. Bureaucratic reorganization typically sees the authorities of one player transferred or duplicated with the creation of a new one. The arrival of a new organization poses a power drain to a monolith like the FBI, which could lose authorities, funding, or personnel to newcomers. Studying the development of the FBI as the lead federal agency for domestic counterterrorism is a precondition for understanding later changes to the U.S. counterterrorism system. An examination of the FBI's history, culture, and changing mission in the fight against terrorism shows the challenges of the rigid FBI, and by extension federal government, to adapt to the dynamic threat of terrorism.

Building the FBI

The Federal Bureau of Investigation traces its birthday to July 26, 1908 as then-U.S. Attorney General Charles J. Bonaparte battled legislators to create his own force of investigators to support the Department of Justice's (DOJ) growing mandate.[1] These investigators would later become known as the FBI and would

eventually become the premier U.S. federal law enforcement agency. Understanding

the FBI's birth and its culture means acknowledging parallels between the early FBI's

growth and its growing counterterrorism mission that developed in the 1980s. In each

instance, the DOJ and FBI were influenced by power struggles with the U.S.

Congress.

Prior to having dedicated investigators, the DOJ had borrowed personnel from

the Department of Treasury's U.S. Secret Service, an unusual arrangement that ended

after a rebuke from Congress.[2] Mistrust grew to the point where "fears were

expressed that the Secret Service was spying on the private lives of members of

Congress."[3] President Roosevelt used an executive order to create the FBI, then

known as the "bureau of investigation" to skirt Congressional opposition.[4] The

contentious relationship between the FBI and the U.S. Congress would continue to

shape the institution as it saw massive growth in the 20th Century that included a

reputation for success, but not without controversy.

Several decades later, the FBI again faced criticism from Congress and drew

public outcry for the reach of its investigators, a crisis that shaped their experience in

the lead up to September 11, 2001. In the wake of the 1974 Watergate scandal,

Senator Frank Church led the Special Select Committee to Investigate Intelligence

Activities, also known as the Church Committee, targeted the Central Intelligence

---

[1] Rhodri Jeffreys-Jones, *The FBI: A History* (New Haven, CT: Yale University Press, 2007), 39.
[2] Ibid., 49.
[3] Ibid.
[4] Ibid., 50.

Agency (CIA) and FBI for abuses of power.[5] In response to FBI investigations on more than 500,000 "subversives" that yielded no convictions, FBI efforts to incite violence among African Americans, and a counterintelligence program that harassed civil rights and anti-Vietnam War activists, the Church Committee moved to check FBI power.[6] Professor Loch K. Johnson, a former Special Assistant to the Chair of the Senate Intelligence Committee, notes:

> The committee's central conclusion was clear and important: The law works. In every case where the secret agencies had violated the law, the committee demonstrated how U.S. security objectives could have been achieved through legal means. As the committee emphasized, security and liberty are compatible values in a democracy; it is possible to defend the nation without becoming a police state.[7]

In sum, the FBI's illegal investigative activities in the Vietnam Era opened the door for intense and justified Congressional oversight. The mounting effort to shield civil liberties, however, made vulnerable the country's ability to protect lives. As the Congress sought greater oversight of the FBI, they also created an organizational obstacle to sharing law enforcement and intelligence data, introducing the conditions for a more stove-piped national security establishment.

Early Success Against Terrorism

Perhaps eager to showcase the good deeds of the FBI and the larger Justice Department, the FBI adjusted its focus and touted its newfound successes in the 1980s. Turning its attention to tangible threats like the Weather Underground, the Black Liberation Army, and the Armed Forces of National Liberation, the FBI

---

[5] Loch K. Johnson, "Congressional Supervision of America's Secret Agencies: The Experience and Legacy of the Church Committee," *Public Administration Review* 64, no. 1 (January/February 2004): 11-12.

[6] Ibid., 6.

[7] Ibid., 11-12.

rehabilitated its reputation by pursuing violent domestic extremists with the support

of lawmakers.[8] Leveraging these conditions, the agency raised its counterterrorism

program from Priority 3 to Priority 1 and Attorney General William French Smith

issued new guidelines for domestic security and terrorism investigations.[9] What

happened next is likely a combination of factors. A newly confident FBI emerged

from a dark chapter in its history by bringing to justice several dangerous groups that

threatened Americans. With these notable victories, the FBI's counterterrorism

successes became inflated, and it defaulted to a new standard of fighting terrorists

through criminal investigation and prosecution.

As the agency refined its forensic investigation expertise and showed an

unparalleled ability to track down domestic extremists, it further reestablished its

identity as premier law enforcement agency that isolated its limited intelligence

mandate. Detailing the environment during the 1990s, the 9/11 Commission Report

notes:

> Responsibility for domestic intelligence gathering on terrorism was vested
> solely in the FBI, yet during almost all of the Clinton administration the
> relationship between the FBI Director and the President was nearly
> nonexistent. The FBI Director would not communicate directly with the
> President. His key personnel shared very little information with the
> National Security Council and the rest of the national security community.
> As a consequence, one of the critical relationships in the counterterrorism
> effort was broken.[10]

In part reacting to the negative consequences of its last encounter with domestic

intelligence, and partly due to the lack of perceived threat, the FBI embraced

---

[8] Brent L. Smith, *Terrorism in America: Pipe Bombs and Pipe Dreams* (Albany, NY: State University of New York Press, 1994), 9.
[9] Ibid., 10.
[10] National Commission on Terrorist Attacks Upon the United States, *Final Report of the National Commission on Terrorist Attacks Upon the United States*, Government Printing Office (Washington, DC, 2004), 358.

independent investigations and prosecutions. Secrecy defined the FBI's law enforcement culture, but ran counter to its counterterrorism responsibilities.

Ultimately, the FBI evolved without the tools or culture to fight the terrorist threat of the late 20th Century. Daniel Byman of the Brookings Institution sums up that "the FBI still thinks in terms of cases, and the organization still focuses on prosecution over prevention."[11] In short, accomplishments of the 1980s and 1990s shaped a new paradigm for the FBI, which further entrenched a culture ill-equipped to fight the new threat of Islamic extremism. Both organizational structure and legislative limitations smothered the FBI's evolution, adding to the cultural barriers. With a system that saw the more than fifty FBI field offices operate in near-vacuums and political sensitivities to investigating religious-based terrorism, the FBI found itself backed into a corner.[12] In congressional testimony in 2000, Norman J. Rabkin with the then General Accounting Office – now Government Accountability Office (GAO) – cautioned about the FBI's "strict legal limitations on the collection and use of intelligence data."[13]

Despite these institutional obstacles to growth, leaders in Washington relied on the FBI to lead the counterterrorism charge. Presidential Decision Directive 39, issued in the wake of the Oklahoma City bombing, formalized the FBI's role as lead federal agency for domestic terrorism incidents.[14] The agency's record during the 1990s was inflated and its confidence was boosted by a series of high-profile

---

[11] Daniel Byman, *The Five Front War: The Better Way to Fight Global Jihad* (Hoboken, NJ: John Wiley & Sons, 2008), 147.

[12] Ibid., 146.

[13] General Accounting Office (GAO), *Combating Terrorism: Linking Threats to Strategies and Resources, by Norman J. Rabkin, Director National Security Preparedness Issues, GAO* (Washington, DC: Government Printing Office, 2000), 7.

[14] General Accounting Office (GAO), *Combating Terrorism: Issues to Be Resolved to Improve Counterterrorism Operations, by the GAO* (Washington, DC: Government Printing Office, 1999), 5.

prosecutions and convictions. Adept at solving complex cases after incidents had occurred, the FBI's management did not focus on preemptive investigations to catch terrorists in the act. The lead federal agency title was something of a misnomer as the FBI directed independent investigations in a reactive pattern rather than building a national model with a Whole-of-Government approach. Prior to 9/11, this effort failed to fully address the totality of these events that translated into a greater threat to national security. In reviewing federal leadership combating terrorism, a 2000 GAO report questioned the wisdom of both the National Security Council and FBI developing independent national counterterrorism strategies.[15] Specifically citing the confusion and frustration of state and local governments, this report foreshadowed future complications in relations between Washington and its state and local counterparts.

Discordant relations with the U.S. Congress and a culture of independence shaped the FBI's early years as a law enforcement agency that resembled both a national police and a domestic intelligence agency, but served as neither. Assuming the role of lead federal agency for domestic counterterrorism in 1995 changed little in the FBI's approach, and the relatively weak executive order gave no real power over state or local governments.[16] Instead, the FBI perfected a few pieces of the counterterrorism process – responding to terrorism with investigations and prosecutions – without really providing leadership in counterterrorism as a national

---

[15] Rabkin, 8.

[16] Presidential Decision Directive-39 (PDD-39) identified the Department of State as the LFA for overseas terrorism and the FBI as the LFA for domestic terrorism. PDD-39 reiterated earlier statutory responsibilities of the Director of the FBI as the "head of investigative agency for terrorism," in U.S. President, *Presidential Decision Directive 39: U.S. Policy on Counterterrorism* (Washington, DC: Government Printing Office, June 21, 1995).

security issue. Poor communication between the FBI and other stakeholders in the months leading to 9/11 demonstrated that even the FBI juggernaut did not have all of the information or tools to prevent catastrophe.

Perhaps in response to the FBI's historical approach to counterterrorism, the 2011 Presidential Policy Directive 8: National Preparedness offers insight into the current administration's interpretation of the FBI's role. This document charges the Secretary of Homeland Security with "coordinating the domestic all-hazards preparedness efforts" that includes "prevention, protection, mitigation, response, and recovery."[17] Since PPD-8 does not explicitly mention the FBI role, but addresses the role of other departments and agencies in general, it follows that the FBI's lead federal agency role in counterterrorism applies mostly to an investigative mandate. DHS, on the other hand, has a supporting role in investigations, but a primary role in prevention, building resilience, and dealing with the aftermath of terrorist attacks.

As the designated lead federal agency for domestic counterterrorism, the FBI remains the starting point for discussing the issue as a part of a larger national security framework. Despite this lead title, the FBI represents only one of many actors in the counterterrorism community. A contentious relationship with the American public and the Congress has constrained the FBI's reach and fostered the development of a culture averse to sharing or blending law enforcement and intelligence roles. Though an undisputed expert in investigations that supported terrorist prosecutions, an FBI revolution only began following September 11, 2001.

---

[17] U.S. President, *Presidential Policy Directive 8: National Preparedness* (Washington DC: Government Printing Office, March 30, 2011), 4.

Subsequent chapters will discuss the agency's performance since its reorganization, and the way forward for the wider counterterrorism enterprise.

CHAPTER 3: COORDINATING BODIES AND SPECIALIZED AGENCIES

Introducing the Field

Paralleling the model of a separation of powers between legislative, executive, and judicial branches, the American counterterrorism domain is a crowded field of actors with varying mandates and designs. While Chapter 2 introduced a leading player in the FBI, Chapter 3 identifies and explains the roles of the supporting cast. Appraising the roles of the National Security Council, the Homeland Security Council, the Department of Homeland Security, and the Office of the Director of National Intelligence provides greater perspective to the forthcoming case studies. The study reveals four diverse organizations that differ in scope, but have overlapping responsibilities; consequently, understanding the national counterterrorism environment is an untidy endeavor. Since most of these bodies were established post 9/11, a review of their performance and interrelations colors the current state of counterterrorism efforts.

The National Security Council (NSC) & Homeland Security Council (HSC)

Established in 1947, The NSC is designed to advise the President on the integration of domestic, foreign, and military policy and to enable better cooperation across the federal government in matters of national security.[1] The NSC in its current form includes two parts: NSC Principals, or statutory members like the Secretary of State

---

[1] Congressional Research Service, *The National Security Council: An Organizational Assessment, by Richard A. Best, Jr., Specialist in National Defense, Congressional Research Service, December 28, 2011* (Washington, DC: Government Printing Office, 2011), 1.

and Secretary of Defense, and the recently renamed National Security Staff (NSS).[2] A

branch of the Executive Office of the President, the entire NSC organization is roughly

250 people tasked with major efforts and only limited infrastructure.[3]   The Central

Intelligence Agency (CIA) Center for the Study of Intelligence best describes the

sweeping mandate, but small footprint of the body:

> The NSC staff is organized into regional and functional directorates
> located in the Old Executive Office Building (OEOB). A directorate is
> headed by a Senior Director, who is appointed by the President to
> coordinate and oversee Presidential policy in a particular area. A Senior
> Director's counterpart at State or Defense would be at the Assistant
> Secretary level. The Senior Director supports the National Security
> Adviser, in effect coordinating the interagency policy agenda in a given
> area. The directorates are best described as a mile wide and an inch deep
> because they usually consist only of a Senior Director assisted by two to
> four directors.[4]

This description shows the scale of a Senior Director's office, in some cases perhaps

three people working on a functional directorate like Global Development, Stabilization,

and Humanitarian Assistance, compared to its equivalent Assistant Secretary, which may

have hundreds or thousands of employees. While proximate to power and largely

influential, the NSC as an organization lacks the mandate or personnel to perform like the

Department of State or Department of Defense. In judging how the NSC drives policy

coordination and leadership across a diverse counterterrorism enterprise, this factor will

be particularly relevant.

---

[2] Laura Rozen, "Introducing the National Security Staff," Politico,
http://www.politico.com/blogs/laurarozen/0110/Introducing_the_National_Security_Staff.html (accessed
January 10, 2013).
    [3] Spencer S. Hsu, "Obama Integrates Security Councils, Adds New Offices, " *The Washington
Post*, May 27, 2009.
    [4] Michael Donley, Cornelius O'Leary, and John Montgomery, "Inside the White House Situation
Room: A National Nerve Center," Central Intelligence Agency Center for the Study of Intelligence,
https://www.cia.gov/library/center-for-the-study-of-intelligence/csi-publications/csi-
studies/studies/97unclass/whithous.html (accessed January 10, 2013).

The NSC's reach is often personality-driven since its broad coordinating authority means it potentially influences the direction of many cabinet departments, but ultimately does not own key processes. Strong National Security Advisors (NSA) have occasionally corralled State and Defense, with Henry Kissinger taking it to the extreme serving concurrently as NSA and Secretary of State, but an effective counterterrorism system cannot rely on personalities alone. The Congressional Research Service explains that "concerns about executive branch oversight of the U.S. response to transnational threats led to the 1996 passage of amendments to the National Security Act of 1947," which indicated problems with information sharing and coordination persisted despite international terrorism inching closer to the United States.[5] The reorganization proved to be a minor course correction rather than a change in thinking, and the failure to acknowledge the signs of an impending attack in the fall of 2001 finally jumpstarted major structural changes.

The 9/11 Commission found that rivalry among competing agencies left the NSC saddled with the lead in joint operational planning for national counterterrorism efforts, stretching its manpower and design.[6] Further, the commission noted caution is needed when White House staff – largely beyond Congressional oversight – directly manages operations; consequently, working these issues also detracts from advising the President on large-scale policy issues.[7] On October 29, 2001, President Bush issued an executive order creating the Homeland Security Council (HSC) in an attempt to refocus

---

[5] Congressional Research Service, *Intelligence and Law Enforcement: Countering Transnational Threats to the U.S., by Richard A. Best, Jr., Specialist in National Defense, Congressional Research Service, December 3, 2001* (Washington, DC: Government Printing Office, 2001), 20.

[6] National Commission on Terrorist Attacks Upon the United States, *Final Report of the National Commission on Terrorist Attacks Upon the United States*, Government Printing Office (Washington, DC, 2004), 402.

[7] Ibid.

counterterrorism efforts in a structure similar to and parallel to the NSC.[8] This

experiment lasted only 8 years as the Obama Administration merged the staffs of the

NSC and HSC "to speed up and unify security policymaking inside the White House."[9]

While a separate HSC exists at the principals' level, one staff supports both structures

and effectively eliminates a potential wall being created between issues of homeland and

national security.

Arguably powerful, but limited in focus and action, the NSC is central to

improving counterterrorism policy and structure. As the "highest coordinative body and

advisory body within the Government aside from the President's Cabinet" the NSC's

future remains contingent on each President's personal management style. Many agree

the NSC should play a larger role in counterterrorism, but in what precise form is unclear.

Though vested with significant power, the NSC cannot develop expert policy and advice

for the President and simultaneously manage operations.

The Department of Homeland Security (DHS)

On January 24, 2003, DHS became the newest cabinet department of the federal

government, a direct response to the terrorist attacks of September 11, 2001.[10] Prior to its

founding, "homeland security activities were spread across more than 40 federal agencies

and an estimated 2,000 Congressional appropriations accounts.[11] This sweeping

reorganization of government bureaucracy faced challenges from the very start. The

department's sheer size and scope coupled with its broad mission created controversy and

---

[8] Congressional Research Service, *Presidential Directives: Background and Overview, by Harold C. Relyea, Specialist in American National Government, Congressional Research Service, February 10, 2003* (Washington, DC: Government Printing Office, 2003), 7.
[9] Hsu.
[10] U.S. Department of Homeland Security, History Office, *Brief Documentary History of the Department of Homeland* Security, Government Printing Office (Washington, DC, 2008), 10.
[11] Ibid., 3.

growing pains detracted from its performance. In a major investigative series exploring

the birth of DHS, *The Washington Post* stated:

> To some extent, the department was set up to fail. It was assigned the
> awesome responsibility of defending the homeland without the
> investigative, intelligence and military powers of the FBI, CIA and the
> Pentagon; it was also repeatedly undermined by the White House that
> initially opposed its creation. But the department has also struggled to
> execute even seemingly basic tasks, such as prioritizing America's most
> critical infrastructure.[12]

Evolving out of the White House Office of Homeland Security, DHS seemed to illustrate

a half-effort, creating a counterterrorism watchdog, but leaving it without much power.

Management issues aside, DHS struggled to define itself among a collection of power

players in the national security scheme. In the decade that has passed, few Americans

associate DHS with anything but inconvenient security screening at airports and scathing

reports calling for the DHS to be disbanded.

Reversal of negative trends may be on the horizon with the Obama

Administration's changes to the DHS model, and a sense of continuity provided by DHS

Secretary Janet Napolitano's tenure entering an unprecedented second term in the

position. Former Obama Homeland Security official Juliette Kayyem argues that U.S.

federalism limits the DHS mandate to coordinate among "50 governors all kings unto

themselves."[13] With experience working as a state homeland security official as well,

Kayyem believes that "[t]he terrorist attacks on 9/11 and the fear that animated so many

decisions then made us forget this obvious fact: As a nation, we are built unsafe."[14]

Although federalism poses challenges to integrating and unifying effort, the United States

---

[12] Susan B. Glasser and Michael Grunwald, "Prelude to Disaster: The Making of DHS
_ Department's Mission Was Undermined from Start," *The Washington Post*, December 22,
2005.
[13] Juliette Kayyem, "Never Say 'Never Again'," Foreign Policy,
http://www.foreignpolicy.com/articles/2012/09/10/never_say_never_again?print=yes&hidecomments=yes
&page=full (accessed October 26, 2012).
[14] Kayyem.

has successfully leveraged federalism to its benefit over the course of its history. While Kayyem exposes a gap in federalism that needs to be addressed, it is not necessarily an inherent vulnerability.

As this paper analyzes a maturing DHS it must also consider the challenges posed by federalism and the constraints DHS faces when judging its contributions to national counterterrorism. Though still in its infancy, and frustrated by overlapping responsibilities without concurrent authorities, the size and budget of DHS alone make it central to discussions going forward. This paper revisits DHS later in a detailed analysis of the DHS grant program as a case study to examine the department's approach.

The Office of the Director of National Intelligence (ODNI) & National Counterterrorism Center (NCTC)

In February 2005, President Bush nominated Ambassador John Negroponte to serve as the first Director of National Intelligence, a position established the year before in the 2004 Intelligence Reform and Terrorism Prevention Act of 2004.[15] The DNI replaced the Central Intelligence Agency Director (then DCI) as the head of the U.S. Intelligence Community (IC) and "has greater authority over budgetary and personnel decisions across the entire…U.S. intelligence community than that which was possessed by the DCI."[16] The office's creation immediately drew criticism of adding a new layer of bureaucracy and speculation of new turf wars, particularly with the displaced CIA Director. Like DHS, DNI too faced an already crowded and entrenched U.S. government

---

[15] *Intelligence Reform and Terrorism Prevention Act of 2004*, Public Law 108-458, 108th Cong., (December 17, 2004).

[16] The National Security Archive, "From Director of Central Intelligence to Director of National Intelligence," George Washington University, http://www.gwu.edu/~nsarchiv/NSAEBB/NSAEBB144/index.htm (accessed January 14, 2013).

culture and an array of agencies with overlapping fiefdoms. Later chapters will explore

the benefits of this redundancy to highlight potential strengths and weaknesses.

With different motivations than the creation of DHS, the ODNI stems from a 9/11

Commission recommendation that also supported relieving the NSC of daily

counterterrorism operations in favor of creating the NCTC.[17] The NCTC was an answer

to old models with information stove pipes, aimed at housing "joint operational planning

and joint intelligence" with a multiagency staff.[18] Uniquely, approximately 60% of the

NCTC staff are detailed from other federal agencies and the NCTC Director, confirmed

by the Senate and rank equivalent of a Cabinet Deputy Secretary, reports "to the DNI for

analyzing an integrating information pertaining to terrorism (except domestic terrorism),

for NCTC budget and programs; [while] for planning and progress of joint

counterterrorism operations (other than intelligence operations) he reports directly to the

President."[19] On the surface these two attributes seem to add confusion and uncertainty

to the NCTC, but a closer examination reveals a counterargument.

The NCTC's unusual staffing pattern and dual-reporting requirements support its

status as a novel approach to U.S. counterterrorism planning and organization. An

organization that relies on a staff comprised of more than half detailees from other

agencies offers both positives and negatives. On one hand, the NCTC cuts through

bureaucracy and information sharing issues because analysts from across the Intelligence

Community can reach back to their home organization. Alternately, employing detailees

---

[17] National Commission on Terrorist Attacks Upon the United States, 403.
[18] National Counterterrorism Center, "About the National Counterterrorism Center," National Counterterrorism Center, http://www.nctc.gov/about_us/about_nctc.html (accessed August 17, 2012).
[19] Congressional Research Service, *The National Counterterrorism Center (NCTC) – Responsibilities and Potential Congressional Concerns*, by Richard A. Best, Specialist in National Defense, Congressional Research Service, December 19, 2011 (Washington, DC: Government Printing Office, 2011), 4-6.

can mean less continuity and increased turnover that threatens efficiency. Interestingly, the functions performed at the NCTC belong to DHS by statute, but were not assigned there because of "considerable concern that DHS, as a new agency and not a longtime member of the Intelligence Community, would not be the place for the integration of highly sensitive information from multiple government agencies."[20] NCTC, founded a year after DHS, potentially skirts these concerns because it employs so many detailees whose home agencies trust to manage their proprietary data. A second foundation for the NCTC's success is a direct line to the President, which ensures relevance and an ability to reach the highest levels to obtain decisions, support, and resources in furtherance of its mission.

With growing staffs, budgets, and power, the ODNI and its subordinate NCTC continue to find their niche in the wider U.S. counterterrorism sphere. Both have drawn harsh criticism for their role in the December 25, 2009 incident involving Umar Farouk Abdulmatallab, the so-called "underwear bomber" who threatened a Detroit-bound aircraft.[21] This incident did not feature a failure to share information, but rather a failure to analyze key links among existing information.[22] One incident alone does not undue the progress made in attempting to create dynamic new centers to support overall counterterrorism efforts. In the struggle to reform existing organizational culture, simply creating new organizations is one solution being explored with the creation of DNI and NCTC. The 9/11 Commission recommended that the NCTC have the authority to plan the counterterrorism activities of other agencies, but it is not clear the NCTC has acquired

---

[20] Ibid., 3.
[21] Ibid., 8.
[22] Ibid.

that much depth or reach in its infancy.[23] In looking at a model to consolidate and strengthen U.S. counterterrorism efforts, perhaps the NCTC is a more obvious choice for Lead Federal Agency for counterterrorism while the FBI remains the investigative lead.

Having addressed the many actors and environment of the U.S. counterterrorism enterprise, the discussion turns to what unifies this assorted bureaucracy. With a history of expansion and not contraction, size and complexity bring many resources to the fight against terror while also threatening to undermine the overall effort. Competing agencies with diverse authorities, missions, and histories contribute to a messy web of responsibility for protecting the homeland. However, overlapping mandates eliminates explicit seams and offers redundancy, which can translate to better protections for the public. Strong leadership and developed partnerships are therefore necessary to harness the benefits of this complex system and downplay the potential negatives.

Subsequent chapters will present detailed analyses of three diverse counterterrorism environments through the lens of two considerations: how to best improve interagency coordination and what more equal partnerships will look like. These case studies strive not for an explicit response to these considerations, but rather to better define the U.S. counterterrorism landscape with a truly-consolidated Lead Federal Agency, and a system that utilizes the all-of-Nation instruments of power through more equal partnerships with state and local governments.

---

[23] National Commission on Terrorist Attacks Upon the United States, 406.

CHAPTER 4: THE NEW YORK CITY POLICE DEPARTMENT (NYPD): A BOTTOM-UP APPROACH

Lessons from an Outlier

As the epicenter of the September 11th attacks, New York dominates discussions of U.S. efforts to combat terrorism. Bridging New York's counterterrorism experience with those of other local governments presents challenges because the city is not representative of the average municipality. For this reason, critics may ask what lessons this standout city can offer for refining overall U.S. counterterrorism policy. This chapter argues that New York's independence and outlier status acts as a check and balance on the federal government's monopoly on combating terrorism. As the New York City Police Department (NYPD) has charted its own path, soliciting federal help when necessary or convenient, it has also challenged the premise that the federal government dictates counterterrorism policy. The goal of this case study, which traces the NYPD's transformation into a counterterrorism giant, is to survey the NYPD model's success and apply lessons learned to the counterterrorism efforts of fellow state and local law enforcement as well as wider U.S. counterterrorism policy.

This analysis of the NYPD's transformation in the wake of September 11, 2001 comes in four parts. First, this case study will detail what makes New York unique in order to explain its attractiveness to terrorists in the 1990s and understand the nature of its response to terrorism. Following this vital background, attention turns to the September 11th attack and its immediate implications for the city. Studying the reactions to the attacks amidst the ongoing first responder activity highlights an unprecedented challenge for an American municipality. The third part of this study outlines the NYPD's rapid revolution of its force and mission. It explores a new relationship with the federal government, the creation of its own intelligence service, and the establishment of permanent NYPD presence overseas. Finally, by compiling lessons learned from successes and failures, this case study elicits adaptable best practices to supplement the U.S. counterterrorism enterprise. This approach emphasizes not simply duplicating programs, but focuses on the positive outcomes of the NYPD's provocative engagements with the federal government and its streamlined operations.

A center of commerce, diversity, entertainment, culture, and dynamism, New York City occupies a special place in the world, beyond its status in the United States. Author Brian Nussbaum terms New York a "global city" while building on the concept of World City Theory[1] to understand the city's international character and significance with respect to economic, social and cultural attributes.[2] A key characteristic for New York under this framework is "the growing autonomy of the world city both from regional authority but more so from national authority."[3] In short, New York's reach into the global community is neither constrained by administrative boundaries nor by the United States government. This unique status provides context for the aggressive targeting of New York by extremists as well as the city's fiercely independent response to September 11, 2001, which is discussed later in this chapter.

---

[1] Global or World Cities are critical metropolitan areas with economic, cultural, and social importance that underpin the global economy In Brian Nussbaum, "Protecting Global Cities: New York, London, and the Internationalization of Municipal Policing for Counter Terrorism," *Global Crime* 8, no. 3 (August 2007): 216.

[2] Ibid., 214.

[3] Ibid., 217.

Terror Targets New York

New York's place as a global city substantiates the determination of terrorists seeking to attack not only the United States, but also the West. The symbolism of striking America on perceived safe ground, particularly at the World Trade Center, a marvel of engineering and economic might, brought New York into focus in the early 1990s. In a 1993 report, the Federal Bureau of Investigation (FBI) noted that "for the first time since the end of 1983, there have been two acts of international terrorism within two years conducted inside the United States."[4] Both incidents – the 1992 takeover of the Iranian Mission to the United Nations and the 1993 World Trade Center bombing – occurred in New York, perhaps indicating an ideological shift, but in the very least exposing a new vulnerability in the global city. The 1992 assault on the Iranian Mission, which involved five members of the transnational terrorist group Mujahedin-E-Khalq (MEK), represented one of several nearly simultaneous attacks against Iranian diplomatic establishments across the world on April 5, 1992.[5] Though no evidence links MEK to Osama bin Laden or Al-Qaeda, the complexity of these MEK attacks foreshadowed future sensational and simultaneous attacks on targets around the world by other terror groups.

The case of the Iranian Mission takeover raises three important points. One, neither the NYPD, the FBI, nor the nation appeared to draw larger lessons from this incident. Although directed at the diplomatic mission of an unfriendly Iranian regime lacking formal relations with the United States, the wider context of this attack was

---

[4] U.S. Department of Justice, Federal Bureau of Investigation, *Terrorism in the United States – 1993*, Terrorist Research and Analytical Center, National Security Division, Government Printing Office (Washington, DC, 1994), 26.

[5] Robert D. McFadden, "Iran Rebels Hit Missions in 10 Nations," *The New York Times*, April 6, 1992.

missed. Several Iranian nationals residing in the United States or Canada carried out an attack coordinated with confederates in several Western countries, avoiding detection and prevention by the authorities. Next, the limited effects of property damage and minor injuries eroded attention from the alarming tactics that had been employed. Listing the conviction of the Iranians on minor federal charges that resulted in sentences of only three months incarceration under the heading of "Significant Accomplishments" in the 1993 Terrorism in United States report, the incident failed to prompt a serious inquiry or reaction from the U.S. government to adapt to a nascent threat.[6] Finally, the group's ability to blend into New York's diverse population and avoid detection would become a familiar modus operandi of terror cells in the United States for the next decade. Failure to recognize these attributes of the threat hampered U.S. attempts to prevent and interdict groups employing similar tactics a few years later.

Early Responses to Terror

The 1993 World Trade Center bombing and subsequent discovery of a conspiracy targeting the United Nations, the massive federal building at 26 Federal Plaza, and the Lincoln and Holland Tunnels reaffirmed the dichotomy between terrorism and U.S. counterterrorism policy. As the terrorism threat grew, the counterterrorism approach stagnated and failed to adapt. Through the lens of hindsight, the previously-referenced FBI report on terrorism in 1993 shows how U.S. institutions were not blind to the threat:

> The most notable development in 1993 was the emergence of international radical fundamentalism both around the world and inside the United States. The bombing of the World Trade Center and the terrorism preventions in New York City are manifestations of this new phenomena.[7]

---

[6] U.S. Department of Justice, Federal Bureau of Investigation, 5.
[7] Ibid., 26.

The real challenge existed in interpreting the context of the threat, avoiding drawing false lessons learned, and shifting the counterterrorism emphasis from prosecution to prevention. Without a new paradigm for proactively disrupting terror cells, the United States' answer to this evolving threat was to use old tools that were proven to fight the old enemy.

Much like the attack on the Iranian Mission a year earlier, the response to the first World Trade Center bombing appeared to focus on the relatively benign impact of the attacks, not the potential. Indeed, "the World Trade Center bombing in New York killed six and wounded about 1,000, but the terrorists' goal was to topple the twin towers, killing tens of thousands of people.[8] Unfortunately, this attack alone did not propel the counterterrorism debate to the forefront of national politics, possibly because the law enforcement response appeared flawless. The FBI led the robust interagency team in processing a crime scene of unprecedented size and complexity in just one month.[9] With the crime scene processed, and several perpetrators due to stand trial, law enforcement seemingly completed its work and few attempted to dig deeper at the root causes or backers of the attack. NYPD Police Commissioner during the World Trade Center bombing, Ray Kelly explained, "There was the assumption that the federal government was taking care of business, and, you know, that was true in '93…that gave us, I think, a false sense of security that we really had this threat under control.[10] Kelly's impressions

---

[8] U.S. National Commission on Terrorism, *Countering the Changing Threat of International Terrorism: Report of the National Commission on Terrorism*, Government Printing Office (Washington, DC, 2000).

[9] U.S. Department of Justice, Federal Bureau of Investigation, 25.

[10] Christopher Dickey, *Securing The City: Inside America's Best Counterterror Force – The NYPD* (New York, NY: Simon & Schuster, 2009), 16.

during his first tour as commissioner colored his perspective close to a decade later when he returned to the job in 2002, determined to learn from the past.

As discussed earlier, the 1993 World Trade Center bombing served notice to the world that international terrorists had not only the desire, but also the reach to strike the U.S. homeland. Although the investigative response and subsequent prosecutions marked victories for the Department of Justice, the United States did not adjust its focus from reaction to prevention soon enough. New York's leaders followed a similar path, but the foundations for an even greater independent streak grew even before 2001.

On June 7, 1999, New York Mayor Rudolph W. Giuliani unveiled a $13 million emergency operations center at 7 World Trade Center.[11] It can be argued that following a progressively terror-filled 1990s that saw attacks on the federal building in Oklahoma City and the bombings of the U.S. embassies in Kenya and Tanzania, the center's opening made sense. New York's federal court had hosted four major terrorism trials between 1994 and 1997, and the United States Attorney's Office for the Southern District of New York and its law enforcement partners were soon the nation's experts in terrorism investigations and prosecutions.[12]

New York After 9/11: An NYPD Revolution

In the weeks following the September 11th attacks, transition dominated the national psyche. From peace to war; defensive to offensive; reactive to proactive; the entire country, and world perhaps, recognized that the United States was vulnerable and that change was on the horizon. On the micro-level, change in New York City began

---

[11] Judith Miller, "With Crisis in Mind, Center Opens," *The New York Times*, June 8, 1999.
[12] Mary Jo White, "Prosecuting Terrorism in New York," *Middle East Quarterly* 8, no. 2 (Spring 2001): 12.

more slowly, but quickly overtook federal efforts. A different transition took place in New York for two reasons. First, recovery efforts across the city dominated the NYPD's focus:

> The police went on twelve hour shifts to increase the number of uniformed bodies on the streets. Many officers explained that, with the commute, twelve hour shifts often meant fourteen to sixteen hour days. Sleep deprivation became a frequent topic of conversation. In addition to guarding and directing traffic, they were digging in the destruction of Ground Zero, sifting through the debris, and helping identify bodies. The New York Police Department (NYPD) started spending about $2.2 million per day on overtime – over $200 million in the first three months.[13]

While the federal government's wide reach and responsibility directed its attention to planning the invasion of Afghanistan, New York first had to lead crisis response efforts and swarm the city with police to keep order and avoid another attack.

Additionally, term-limited Mayor Rudolph W. Giuliani became a lame duck several weeks later, so a new strategy for counterterrorism would have to wait. In November 2001, with Mayor-Elect Michael R. Bloomberg preparing for his transition to New York's City Hall, the selection of Ray Kelly as police commissioner translated into the city's first bold move against terrorism. Taking office nearly four months after the attacks, Commissioner Kelly led the Bloomberg Administration's deliberate and agile counterterrorism revolution. Whereas the federal government initially raced towards counterterrorism reform with differing agendas in the legislative and executive branches, New York relied on unified leadership and a smaller bureaucracy that allowed NYPD reform to surpass federal efforts. In doing so, the NYPD began to craft today's highly capable, if not controversial force.

---

[13] Avram Bornstein, "Antiterrorist Policing in New York City after 9/11: Comparing Perspectives on a Complex Process," *Human Organization* 64, no. 1(Spring 2005): 52.

Mistrust and a lack of information drove the NYPD's expansion into intelligence and counterterrorism. Examining Ray Kelly's efforts to build a team of Washington insiders, organizational restructuring of the NYPD, and the development of unique international partnerships shows how NYPD overcame roadblocks to protecting New York. Moreover, a detailed analysis will demonstrate how New York pioneered new approaches of policing and counterterrorism that drew praise from the federal government and international partners.

Losing the effort to pull information from the national security establishment, the NYPD changed course and recruited its own network of informants: Washington insiders with access and hailing from distinguished federal careers. Describing Commissioner Kelly's early mindset, journalist Christopher Dickey explains "Ray Kelly's basic goal was to know everything about *anything* that could threaten New York City."[14] Challenged by layers of bureaucracy, a history of power struggles and resentment among key players, and a position as an outsider looking in, Kelly formed a team of Washington insiders to break the stalemate.[15]

Showing the streamlined process to reorganize and hire without the lengthy federal confirmation process, New York City named retired United States Marine Corps Lieutenant General and former Department of Defense (DOD) Special Assistant for Homeland Security Frank Libutti as the NYPD's first Deputy Commissioner of Counter-Terrorism on January 16, 2002.[16] Only eight days later, David Cohen former Deputy

---

[14] Dickey, 70.

[15] Ibid., 71.

[16] City of New York, "Mayor Michael R. Bloomberg And Police Commissioner Raymond W. Kelly Appoint United States Marine Lieutenant General Frank Libutti in Newly-Created Post of Deputy Commissioner of Counter-Terrorism," Office of the Mayor, http://www.nyc.gov/portal/site/nycgov/menuitem.b270a4a1d51bb3017bce0ed101c789a0/index.jsp?pageID

Director for Operations and 35-year veteran Central Intelligence Agency (CIA) joined the

NYPD as Libutti's counterpart, the Deputy Commissioner for Intelligence.[17]

Commenting on the Cohen's appointment, Mayor Bloomberg explained, "the

world no longer stops at the oceans, our world goes every place, and we have to make

sure we that we get the best information as quickly as we possibly can."[18] Bloomberg's

comments implicitly frame New York's perspective that information did not reach the

city through regular channels, and New York's leaders had just opened new lines of

communication with these hires. The success of this tactic led to its repetition and

growth. With Cohen's connections, he convinced the CIA to detail Lawrence H. Sanchez

– an active CIA employee – exclusively to the NYPD to enshrine the flow of

information.[19] This increased cooperation between the CIA and the NYPD set the

conditions for the NYPD's next endeavor: transformation. With the prerequisite access

to information that no other municipality in the country had, attention turns to the

NYPD's quest to convert the information into a counterterrorism advantage.

Building New York's Counterterrorism Machine

The NYPD grounded its successful response to September 11, 2001 with its agile

reorganization and robust funding of two offices, the Intelligence Division (ID) and

Counter-Terrorism Bureau (CTB).   Once Commissioner Kelly's senior management

team was hired, they moved to reform the ID and mold the complementary CTB for

maximum effect. Prior to 9/11, the Intelligence Division's name was an outright

---

nyc_blue_room&catID=1194&doc_name=http%3A%2F%2Fwww.nyc.gov%2Fhtml%2Fom%2Fhtml%2F
2002a%2Fpr012-02.html&cc=unused1978&rc=1194&ndi=1 (accessed October 29, 2012).
[17] City of New York, "Administration – Intelligence," New York City Police Department,
http://www.nyc.gov/html/nypd/html/administration/intelligence_co.shtml (accessed October 29, 2012).
[18] Dickey, 36-37.
[19] Ibid., 73.

misnomer as it had no intelligence function and mainly consisted of detectives assigned

to accompany visiting foreign dignitaries or VIPs across the city.[20] Seeking to build an

actual intelligence collection and analysis capability, the force hired "a cadre of civilian

analysts [to] provide intelligence and policy support to the NYPD leadership."[21] A

seasoned leader and new hiring authority overcame some of the Intelligence Division's

issues, but these improvements to organization and structure were just the beginning.

Mirroring the federal effort to expand law enforcement and intelligence

authorities that were seen as lacking after 9/11, the NYPD pursued a similar course of

action. In his meticulous account of national security and federalism, Columbia

University's Matthew Waxman details the city's federal court efforts:

> The New York Police Department (NYPD) moved to modify an
> agreement that had emerged in the 1980s out of allegations that its
> intelligence unit had engaged in constitutionally improper surveillance and
> infiltration practices, including improper compilation of vast dossiers on
> individuals. The NYPD argued to the district court that the resulting
> restrictions on intelligence practices now prevented it from using its
> surveillance powers before it was too late to stop an attack.[22]

With a sympathetic court in Lower Manhattan, just blocks away from the World Trade

Center, the ID gained new powers "to proactively monitor public activity and look for

indications of terrorist or criminal activity," no longer subject to an external review

panel.[23] The ID's course here clearly sought to avoid errors of the past; consequently, the

---

[20]Scott Stewart, "Growing Concern Over the NYPD's Counterterrorism Methods," Stratfor Global Intelligence, http://www.stratfor.com/weekly/20111012-growing-concern-over-nypds-counterterrorism-methods (accessed October 26, 2012).

[21] The Washington Institute, "Defending the City: NYPD's Counterterrorism Operations," Policy Watch, http://www.washingtoninstitute.org/policy-analysis/view/defending-the-city-nypds-counterterrorism-operations (accessed October 26, 2012).

[22] Matthew C. Waxman, "National Security Federalism in the Age of Terror," *Stanford Law Review* 64, no. 289 (February 2012): 314.

[23] Stewart.

NYPD had set the conditions for crafting its own intelligence network as prevention became priority number one.

Creating a shadow intelligence agency, Commissioner Kelly oversaw the hiring of more than 600 linguists fluent in 45 languages like Dari, Arabic, Farsi, and Urdu.[24] Proving the expertise of their new talent, the NYPD detailed some of these linguists to federal agencies lacking similar capability after the CIA approached the NYPD about intelligence discovered on the internet by the police force that the CIA had not detected.[25] These examples illustrate the department's ability to leverage its size and budget to create a unique capacity for intelligence gathering. The lesson here is not for Akron, Ohio to emulate New York, but rather that the NYPD's approach demonstrates that municipalities and state governments can supplement the sprawling, yet often incomplete federal response to terrorism. A diverse community with speakers of historically challenging languages plus a departure from stringent federal background investigations, which often exclude these native speakers, proved to be an important contribution to protecting New York.[26]

Acting on the analysis and support from the Intelligence Division, the NYPD Counter-Terrorism Bureau mixes a very public show of force with swarms of investigators to continue the department's emphasis on prevention. The CTB provided the surge in detectives assigned to the Joint Terrorism Task Force (JTTF) following 9/11, an increase from 17 to 130.[27] Kelly's CTB has thrived thanks to a budget reported at

---

[24] Dickey, 141-143.
[25] Brian Nussbaum, "From Brescia to Bin Laden: The NYPD, International Policing, and 'National Security'," *Journal of Applied Security Research* 7, no. 2 (April 2012): 193.
[26] Ibid., 186.
[27] Ibid., 190.

$330 million and a staff of approximately 1,200 personnel.[28] It is noteworthy that

manpower and a hefty budget alone do not equal success since the federal government

tends to bring both resources to national security problems. What Kelly's model does

employ is near-universal support of the Mayor, the New York City Council, and the

public. Kelly recruited experts and professionals to build a new force and "Mayor

Bloomberg supported him; without that support, changes like those undertaken by Kelly

would not have stood a chance of being successful."[29] The NYPD employed better

capabilities than the federal government without being restricted by federal bureaucracy,

responsibilities, and authorities.

Showing no end to the appetite for information, the NYPD's deployment of

detectives overseas as International Liaison Officers (ILOs) was the final cornerstone of a

new counterterrorism strategy. Despite forging an invaluable relationship with the CIA

and creating its own mini-intelligence service, Commissioner Kelly used this opportunity

to collect some of the fastest-breaking threat information while drawing renewed

criticism from the FBI.[30] Evidence of the program's value comes as recently as 2010

when the NYPD announced plans to expand the program beyond liaisons already

deployed in at least 10 countries.[31] Critics argue that a local police department should

not encroach on a federal responsibility, threatening traditional diplomatic exchanges and

introducing redundancy. The NYPD has weathered this criticism thanks to hefty political

---

[28] Judith Miller, "Cross Country: How the NYPD Foiled the Post-9/11 Terror Plots," *The Wall Street Journal*, September 10, 2011.
[29] Nussbaum, "From Brescia to Bin Laden," 200.
[30] Stewart.
[31] Joel Stonington and Sean Gardiner, "NYPD Weighs New Posts Abroad," *The Wall Street Journal*, May 12, 2010.

capital and an unusual funding mechanism that finances the overseas liaisons through the private Police Foundation of New York.[32]

The federalism debate is neither restricted to counterterrorism, nor a new clash between federal and state or local officials, as evidenced by Arizona's S.B. 1070, which required state and local law enforcement to increase illegal immigration enforcement measures in response to perceived inability or apathy of the federal government to do so.[33] Challenged by the Department of Justice, this case went to the U.S. Supreme Court that ruled against Arizona's proactive measure as the Congressional Research Service notes:

> While the majority opinion acknowledged the "importance of immigration policy" to the states, and in particular those, like Arizona, which "bear[] many of the consequences of unlawful immigration," it nonetheless viewed state and local laws to be permissible only to the extent that they are not "in conflict or at cross-purposes" with the immigration framework created by the national government.[34]

Although the Supreme Court's ruling constrained the ability of this state government to take the initiative where it saw a gap in federal response, the case raised the issue to new heights. This case demonstrates that state and local actors may be primed to act where the federal government is either unwilling or unable; consequently, it furthers the argument that U.S. policies thrive from new ideas emanating not only in Washington, but also in the various states and localities.

The relative impunity of the NYPD to operate overseas despite federal concerns shows the rapid shifts in both the politics of terrorism in New York and a new

---

[32] Nussbaum, "From Brescia to Bin Laden," 196.

[33] Congressional Research Service, *Arizona v. United States: A Limited Role for States in Immigration Enforcement, by the Congressional Research Service, September 10, 2012* (Washington, DC: Government Printing Office, 2012), 1-2.

[34] Ibid., 4.

understanding of the global environment. With the memory of September 11th still strong, New York finds itself with few political opponents. Twenty years earlier when the Iranian MEK launched simultaneous international attacks, the NYPD had a tactical response, but no long-term strategy. Under Kelly's leadership and with widespread, though sometimes tacit support, ILOs now funnel information from the scene of overseas terrorist attacks directly back to police headquarters in case these events merit an immediate change in procedures in New York.[35] The victory of the NYPD against its critics here emerges as a theme in its aggressive defense of New York, which carries over into other programs and policies. It also highlights the benefits to the federal government from improved communication and coordination with state and local partners to create a broader national defense mindful of seams between various layers of government.

Understanding how the New York City Police Department forged its counterterrorism structure requires an understanding of the adversity it faced. At the heart of New York's push to expand its intelligence collection and access to federal information were instances of the FBI excluding the NYPD from cases, as seen in the case of convicted Kashmiri-born Iyman Faris, who plotted to attack the Brooklyn Bridge.[36] Collecting its own intelligence by deploying liaisons overseas and hiring a corps of linguists and intelligence analysts addressed some challenges, but not all.

As the NYPD sought to combine its own intelligence with existing federal information, Kelly's lieutenants David Cohen and Michael Sheehan, a former State Department Ambassador-at-Large for Counter Terrorism, pushed for a new capability. In

---

[35] Patrick McGrevey, "Overseas Links Urged for LAPD; A Panel Created by the Mayor Says Local Efforts in the War on Terror Would Benefit from Placing Officers with Foreign Departments," *Los Angeles Times*, September 9, 2006.

[36] Dafna Linzer, "In New York, a Turf War in the Battle Against Terrorism," *The Washington Post*, March 22, 2008.

a protracted struggle to build a facility inside the NYPD Headquarters at One Police Plaza, after six years, the FBI agreed to certify a Sensitive Compartmented Information Facility (SCIF), capable of housing top secret federal information.[37] After a warming of relations between the FBI and the NYPD credited to a meeting between Commissioner Kelly and FBI Director Mueller in 2005, the Washington Post detailed the Assistant Director-in-Charge of the FBI's New York Office, Mark Mershan's position:

> Mershan said senior officials at the FBI opposed giving the NYPD its own Sensitive Compartmented Information Facility (SCIF) because it would have allowed the department to "bypass the FBI and establish its own links with the intelligence community. Clearly that has happened anyway, so I have called David Cohen and told him that we will be pleased to certify the SCIF."[38]

These comments exemplify the change in the relationship between the NYPD and the FBI, but they also present an underlying uneasiness. The outcome is not necessarily a relationship based on amity and trust, but more likely understanding that neither side can afford not to cooperate. This statement really shows the FBI criticizing the NYPD for skirting the system while grudgingly endorsing better information sharing. It is evidence that a legacy of September 11th is a NYPD that is a strong contributor to wider counterterrorism efforts, which helps justify its go-it-alone mentality and insulate the department from retribution.

Challenging the NYPD Response

Looking beyond the scope of the NYPD-FBI relationship, even greater scrutiny of the NYPD's war on terror came in August 2011 as the Associated Press (AP) released an investigative series that charged the NYPD operated a domestic spying program on

---

[37] Ibid.
[38] Ibid.

tenuous legal grounds and with virtually no oversight.[39] While this series generated

widespread attention on the NYPD's previously secret tactics, the department remained

unapologetic about its programs and credits them for stopping at least 14 terror plots

since 9/11.[40] Although concerns about civil liberties and the NYPD conducting

investigations outside of New York City with murky authorities informed a temporary

national debate, the issue largely faded from view. The remarkable ability to weather this

controversy reflects either a tacit admission that the tactics are working or underscores

that there is diminished appetite to argue against counterterrorism practices lest a future

attack prove the critic wrong. In its analysis of the fallout from the AP investigation,

Scott Stewart of private intelligence firm Stratfor explains:

> The New York City Council does not have the same authority to conduct
> classified hearings that the U.S. Congress does when it oversees national
> intelligence activity. And the federal government has limited legal
> authority at the local level. What [New York City Council] Public Safety
> Committee Chairman Vallone and federal government sources are
> implying is that they are not willing to take on oversight responsibilities in
> New York. In other words, while there are concerns about the NYPD's
> activities, they are happy with the way the department is working and
> want to let it continue, albeit with more accountability.[41]

Though the controversy was not without consequence – the AP reported in early 2012

that the CIA had recalled its representative to the NYPD after the CIA Inspector General

ruled the assignment was not cleared through proper channels – the saga has not thwarted

the NYPD's momentum.[42]

---

[39] Associated Press, "AP's Probe into NYPD Intelligence Operations," Associated Press, http://www.ap.org/Index/AP-In-The-News/NYPD (accessed September 10, 2012).

[40] City of New York, "Press Release: Remarks by Police Commissioner Kelly to Fordham Law Alumni, NYPD, http://www.nyc.gov/html/nypd/html/pr/pr_2012_03_03_remarks_to_fordham_law_school_alumni.shtml (accessed October 23, 2012).

[41] Stewart.

[42] Adam Goldman and Matt Apuzzo, "CIA to Pull Officer from NYPD after Internal Probe," *Associated Press*, January 26, 2012.

Despite weathering criticism of its approach, gaps in the NYPD revolution offer lessons for other cities attempting to replicate its success. Charges that tactics violate civil rights of citizens resulted in crippling changes to federal law enforcement and intelligence practices, as discussed in earlier chapters. If such charges are substantiated, the resulting backlash can potentially undermine counterterrorism gains in the present and prevent them in the future. Simply attracting these charges, therefore, is a weakness in New York's efforts to be considered when applying lessons learned to the wider discussion. Another potential weakness is found in frayed relations with the federal government. Although the FBI-NYPD relationship warmed due to personal efforts of outgoing FBI Director Mueller and Commissioner Kelly, a change in personalities could result in slowed cooperation, which neither the FBI nor the NYPD can afford.

Lessons Learned: Applying the Model Beyond New York

While duplicating the NYPD approach in other municipalities is unlikely, lessons emerge from its creative counterterrorism policies. The creation of the city's own intelligence and counterterrorism systems came in response to the symptom of New York feeling abandoned by the federal government. What the NYPD experience provides is a perspective for understanding existing gaps in the interagency process while also offering some adapted best practices for other municipalities and state governments. A review of the key programs initiated by the NYPD since September 11, 2001 and the capabilities they bring to the department highlight areas ripe for improved cooperation with federal authorities. A second key deliverable from this case study is the adaptation of NYPD successes to those lacking its size, budget, and political influence.

New York City's efforts to build its own intelligence and counterterrorism enterprise reflected three major shortcomings in U.S. counterterrorism policy in the days leading up to the September 11th attacks. The assignment of more than 1,000 people and funding of a few hundred million dollars emphasizes the NYPD's belief that counterterrorism in New York was both undermanned and underfunded.[43] Richard Falkenrath, a former NYPD Deputy Commissioner for Counter Terrorism and White House Homeland Security Official confirms this assertion, "The NYPD, rather, has something the federal government lacks: plenary police power, which gives the department a broad ability to maintain public order, and a unique and important role in overall counterterrorism efforts."[44] The creation of a streamlined intelligence collection and analysis organization, complete with a vast body of diverse linguists speaks to dissatisfaction with intelligence sharing and federal bureaucracy. Finally, the deployment of NYPD detectives to international locations reinforces a complete dissatisfaction with information sharing, not only getting real-time threat information, but also working to obtain security clearances for NYPD personnel and build an infrastructure to process and store classified data.[45]

Although Commissioner Kelly's detailed operational changes account for New York's successes in combating terrorism, key lessons derive from the approach to these changes as much as the innovations themselves. Again, buttressed by its wealth of resources, strong backing of its leadership, and political capital, the city campaigned against the federal standard and created an interplay that challenged the assumption of

---

[43] Miller, "Cross Country."
[44] Ibid.
[45] Judith Miller, "FBI vs. The NYPD," *The New York Post*, March 25, 2008.

federal preeminence in combating terrorism. Writing on national security federalism, Professor Matthew Waxman argues for exploiting state and local actors:

> …harnessing state and local institutions for national security may be needed not merely to bolster efforts otherwise naturally in the domain of the federal government, but to address parts of the national security challenge for which state and local institutions are better suited than the federal government could ever be. The leading accounts of federal-local relations and national security do not adequately incorporate these features into their analyses.[46]

Waxman's point underscores the importance of New York's independent streak as furthering the debate on the best formula for counterterrorism in the United States.

Transforming an innovative success story into an adaptable model for widespread use is challenging and not always advisable; consequently, this fact complicates simple repetition of the NYPD model for combating terrorism across the United States. Not every major city, let alone state government, can afford to dedicate hundreds of millions of dollars or more than a thousand employees to guarding against terrorism. Understanding that premise allows for a more reasoned and scaled approach to sharing New York's best practices.

Discussing New York's overseas liaison program, Professor Brian Nussbaum of the Rockefeller School of Public Affairs explains that "certainly few cities have the resources to mirror the approaches taken by New York or London…it is far more likely that cities may undertake smaller regional variations on the theme."[47] Indeed, other police forces from Los Angeles, Chicago, Las Vegas, and Miami already pool resources for counterterrorism under the Urban Areas Security Initiative.[48]

---

[46] Waxman, 322.
[47] Nussbaum, "Protecting Global Cities," 230.
[48] McGrevey.

Exploring New York's experiences with counterterrorism is replete with value. As the unfortunate target of many attacks, the city offers a number of cases for analysis. Moving forward, this paper will judge the results NYPD's campaign against the competing approaches of the Department of Homeland Security and the Joint Terrorism Task Force.

CHAPTER 5: THE DEPARTMENT OF HOMELAND SECURITY (DHS): A TOP-DOWN APPROACH

A case study evaluating The Department of Homeland Security offers a wide-lens view of the federal government's interaction with state and local partners. Looking at this expansive and maturing cabinet department frames the debate on how to best strengthen counterterrorism (CT) efforts on a national level. Earlier, this paper introduced the major federal players in the domestic CT arena including DHS. While DHS is just one of many federal stakeholders, and relatively new compared to the National Security Council and Federal Bureau of Investigation (FBI), it serves as the face of federal efforts in the post-9/11 era. A complete assessment of whether the agency is adequately organized, funded, or empowered to achieve this mission is a larger question beyond the scope of the current analysis. However, questions about the wider DHS mission color this case study, which investigates the merits of a domestic counterterrorism strategy where Washington mandates policy to state and local governments.

Examining the DHS top-down approach demonstrates the weaknesses of the federal bureaucracy in casting a one-size fits all model on a diverse body of state and local governments divided by geography, capabilities, and threat. This analysis depends on detailed examples of DHS shaping federal efforts since its birth in 2003. The discussion begins with sprawling DHS grant programs for state and local partners, focusing on validating these as pathways to preventing terror. What follows is an appraisal of a highly-touted, but maturing network of fusion centers that seeks to bridge the gaps between big government and small. As the fusion center model touches departments of all sizes, it offers an inclusive look at DHS assistance to a diverse sample

of players.   These sections call out the larger failures of these two programs while trying

to capture lessons learned that demonstrate federal leadership in CT must not equate with

federal dominance.

Federal Assistance to State & Local Governments: DHS Grants

Reflecting the delicate balance between federal and state power, DHS primarily

influences local counterterrorism policy through grant programs that supply money for

those communities pursuing federally-prescribed CT goals. Effectively developing

grants to support CT requires clearly stated objectives, understanding of existing

capabilities, and candid threat assessments. Between 2002 and 2010, "Congress has

appropriated an approximate total of $33 billion for state and local homeland security

assistance with an average annual appropriation of $3.7 billion."[1] Since their inception,

these grants have faced a barrage of criticisms, which reflect the uncertain success of the

federal government in directing local inputs that support national counterterrorism policy.

Judging these complaints requires an analysis of five key areas in the grants process:

development, allocation, administration, assessment, and accountability.

Grants Development

Specific background of DHS grant development is not apparent in most homeland

security literature, so a reasoned analysis requires extrapolation from the federal

government's words and deeds. An August 2002 media report stated that the Bush

---

[1] Congressional Research Service, *Department of Homeland Security Assistance to States and Localities: A Summary and Issues for the 111ᵗʰ Congress, by the Congressional Research Service, April 30, 2010* (Washington, DC: Government Printing Office, 2010), 4-5.

Administration's first National Strategy for Homeland Security "asks cash-strapped state and local officials to spend their own funds meeting federal security standards that in some cases haven't been written yet."[2] Although the federal government reimburses state or local governments through certain grant programs, this remark highlights the counterintuitive aspects of the system that was hurriedly implemented following 9/11. In this case, the 2002 National Strategy for Homeland Security noted:

> ...the Department of Homeland Security will establish national standards for emergency response training and preparedness...These standards would also require certain coursework for individuals to receive and maintain certification as first responders and for state and local governments to receive federal grants. The Department would establish a national exercise program designed to educate and evaluate civilian response personnel at all levels of government. It would require individuals and government bodies to complete successfully at least one exercise every year. The Department would use these exercises to measure performance and allocate future resources.[3]

This proposed evaluation system highlights the struggle between acting fast to protect the country and spending responsibly. Assistance programs without effective allocation formulas, metrics for success, or transparent review run the risk of failing for a host of reasons. In its infancy, DHS employed weak and unproven metrics concurrent to aid disbursement undermined the federal government's credibility, and invited waste.

Five years later, the 2007 National Strategy for Homeland Security explained, "...our Nation still faces the challenge of developing tools for assessing our overall security posture and measuring the effectiveness of Federal assistance."[4] This explicit

---

[2]Jeanne Cummings, "States Mend Homeland Security Blanket – Local Governments Set Plans Amid Miscommunication With Washington, Lack of Funds," *The Wall Street Journal*, August 13, 2002.

[3] U.S. President, *National Strategy for Homeland Security* (Washington, DC: Government Printing Office, July 2002), 45.

[4] U.S. President, *National Strategy for Homeland Security,* (Washington, DC: Government Printing Office, October 2007), 45-46.

acknowledgement of failure to create assessment metrics shows a nearly insurmountable

flaw in the grants development stage, but it is also the first step to reform. Similar

concerns about the growth of these grants came as recently as 2012 from two branches of

government. The DHS Inspector General criticized the Federal Emergency Management

Agency (FEMA), the administrator of all DHS grants saying, "FEMA did not have a

system in place to determine the extent that Homeland Security Grant Program funds

enhanced the states' capabilities to prevent, deter, respond to, and recover from terrorist

attacks," in a June 2012 report. [5] Later that year, a U.S. Senate report found "that

taxpayer money spent on homeland security grant programs has not always been spent in

ways obviously linked to terrorism or preparedness," echoing concerns about grant

development and assessments. [6] A major flaw in grant development is metrics to

measure effectiveness chasing grant money after it has been disbursed.

From Fiscal Year (FY) 2003 to FY2006, DHS administered seven major grant

programs to assist state and local governments, two of which are the focus of this effort:

the State Homeland Security Grant Program (SHSGP) and the Urban Area Security

Initiative (UASI). [7] Looking at FY2006 funding alone, SHSGP was allotted $528 million

with another $711 million for UASI[8], equal to 28.5% and 38.4%, respectively, of total

---

[5] U.S. Department of Homeland Security, *The Federal Emergency Management Agency's Requirements for Reporting Homeland Security Grant Program Achievements*, Office of the Inspector General, Government Printing Office (Washington, DC, 2012), 1.

[6] Senator Tom Coburn, *Safety At Any Price: Assessing the Impact of Homeland Security Spending in U.S. Cities*, Government Printing Office (Washington, DC, 2012), 4.

[7] Congressional Research Service, *Department of Homeland Security Grants to State and Local Governments: FY2003 to FY 2006, by the Congressional Research Service, December 22, 2006* (Washington, DC: Government Printing Office, 2006)

[8] In FY 2012, the SHSGP, renamed the State Homeland Security Program (SHSP), had $294 million in funding available and the UASI had over $490 million In U.S. Department of Homeland Security, "Fiscal Year (FY) 2012 Homeland Security Grant Program (HSGP) Frequently Asked Questions (FAQs)," Federal Emergency Management Agency, http://www.fema.gov/pdf/government/grant/2012/fy12_hsgp_faq.pdf (accessed February 12, 2013).

DHS grants appropriations that year.[9] Holding more than two-thirds of the total funding

in this category makes these programs relevant for this analysis. This sample set also

offers contrasting allocation mechanisms with SHSGP mandating minimum funding for

all states and territories while UASI gives DHS discretionary authority to provide

assistance directly to select urban areas.[10] Accordingly, the positives and negatives of

using the states as interlocutors or working directly with the municipalities shape the

discussion of the best formula for counterterrorism success.

Between FY2003 and FY 2006, the SHSGP centered on countering the threat of

Weapons of Mass Destruction (WMD) in the United States:

> SHSGP provides assistance to state and local entities to prepare for
> terrorist attacks involving weapons of mass destruction (WMD). It
> authorizes the purchase of specialized equipment to enhance state and
> local agencies' capability in preventing and responding to WMD incidents
> and other terrorist incidents and provides funds for designing, developing,
> conducting, and evaluating terrorism response exercises.[11]

Although there is scant literature on the development of this particular program, the

heavy focus on WMD is a window into the perceived threat for the nation's leaders in the

post 9/11 environment. The federal government viewed the SHSGP as an avenue to

channel expertise and resources to state and local governments that were responsible for

protecting citizens in the immediate aftermath of a WMD attack.

The SHSGP's specific parameters stem from the Uniting and Strengthening

America by Providing Appropriate Tools Required to Interrupt and Obstruct Terrorism

(USA PATRIOT ACT) Act of 2001, signed on October 26 of that year, which also

---

[9] Congressional Research Service, *Department of Homeland Security Grants to State and Local Governments,* 3.

[10] Ibid., 4.

[11] Ibid.

included provisions for administration and allocation.[12] Coming only weeks after

September 11, 2001, the rushed creation of this costly program may account for its failure

to address the perceived needs of states and cities themselves. Considering the short time

drafting this legislation, it is highly unlikely that a consortium of relevant state or local

actors gave substantive input on this area of grant development in the chaotic weeks after

9/11. With a focus on immediate action, Congress pushed through desperately needed

federal aid without a deep understanding of state or local needs. Similarly, only two days

after the attack, President Bush promised $40 billion dollars in federal aid for the country,

$20 billion for New York City.[13] Both of these steps reinforce the image of a besieged

federal government eager to reassure with funding, but carless about wasteful spending in

the rush to react.

The Urban Area Security Initiative (UASI) "addresses planning, equipment,

training and exercise needs unique to large urban areas to help build a sustainable

capacity to prevent and defend against acts of terrorism."[14] Congress carved out this

program in response to controversy over the minimum funding processes of other grants,

which drew claims of pork barrel spending with DHS funds.[15] The New School

University's Peter Eisinger noted in 2006 that "the only risk-based grant is the UASI,

which is exempt from the Patriot Act's minimum-distribution requirement."[16] Though the

---

[12] *Uniting and Strengthening America by Providing Appropriate Tools Required to Intercept and Obstruct Terrorism (USA PATRIOT ACT) of 2001*, Public Law 107-56, 107th Cong., (October 26, 2001).

[13] National Commission on Terrorist Attacks Upon the United States. *Final Report of the National Commission on Terrorist Attacks Upon the United States*, Government Printing Office (Washington, DC, 2004), 329.

[14] Alice Lipowicz, "A Guide to Where the Grants Are," Special Issue. *Governing* Securing the Homeland (October 2004): 38.

[15] Andrew Lakoff and Eric Klinenberg, "Of Risk and Pork: Urban Security and the Politics of Objectivity," *Theory and Society* 39, no. 5 (September 2010): 509.

[16] Peter Eisinger, "Imperfect Federalism: The Intergovernmental Partnership for Homeland Security," *Public Administration Review* 66, no. 4 (July/August 2006): 540.

program began with an emphasis on risk-based formulas, it cannot be separated from the politics from which it grew. In response to negative publicity from other programs doling out funds to territories like American Samoa at the expense of New York or Washington, the federal government moved in the right direction for the wrong reasons. What started as a program for seven large cities in FY2003 soon grew to a total of 30 eligible cities before spreading to a total of 64 urban areas by FY2010.[17] Following other patterns of federal spending, it seems likely that the funding followed politics rather than threats.

Briefly comparing and contrasting the development of the SHSGP and UASI highlights the major factors influencing these programs. The required minimum funding aspect of SHSGP is not only wasteful, but also disrupts CT improvements in favor of political pandering. While this formula potentially offered all states and territories a common baseline for homeland security, ignoring the absence of threats to many areas, there is no evidence to support SHSGP as unifying capabilities. Next, the SHSGP requirement that funds are disbursed to states, which determine allocation to localities, carries additional risk of funds being used as political tools by state governments. Emerging as a supplement to SHSGP's myopic approach to funding, the UASI began with a seemingly impartial risk-based formula for granting aid. Despite its growth to include nearly ten times as many urban areas from its modest start, the founding principle of extra funds for those at a higher risk is a model to embrace. Additionally, the novel UASI novel approach of bypassing the state capitals and feeding money to municipalities, a positive mechanism worthy of greater exploration.

---

[17] David Rittgers, "Abolish the Department of Homeland Security," The Cato Institute, http://www.cato.org/publications/policy-analysis/abolish-department-homeland-security (accessed September 10 2012).

As the discussion of federal homeland security grant programs continues, the analysis will demonstrate that flaws in grant development foreshadow failures for the grant process at-large. Simply put, substandard grant programs induced early failure and were much more difficult to correct once they became law. Once the federal government began the cash flow, they created a sense of entitlement among grantees and corresponding sense of duty for their political benefactors. As Washington pushes funds to state and local partners, it also seeks to burden-share, but the early DHS grant process did not created a much-needed dialogue, but instead a monologue from Washington.

Grants Allocation

Just as responsible grants development facilitates effectiveness and efficiency, proper grants allocation is essential to obtaining a return on investment and stimulating change. Once funds began flowing from Washington across the United States, the hastily-conceived allocation process proved to facilitate wasteful spending on the wrong things in the wrong places. Cities complained that DHS-mandated purchases were redundant, in part because grants were confined to a one-size-fits-all approach.[18] Detractors of the slow-moving grant process soon found a competing enemy: charges of politically-driven grant allocation, turning homeland security into a new vehicle for pork barrel legislation.[19]

A major failing of DHS grants, thanks to their legislative preconditions, is the disparity in per capita spending that soon became institutionalized.[20] In FY2003, low population density states like Wyoming ($61 per person), Vermont, and North Dakota led

---

[18] John M. Doyle, "Grants for Homeland Security Have Strings Attached, Mayor Says," *Aviation Week's Homeland Security & Defense*, November 5, 2003.

[19] Kate O'Beirne, "Introducing Pork-Barrel Homeland Security," *National Review*, August 11, 2003.

[20] Lakoff and Klinenberg, 508.

the nation in per capita homeland security spending while California ($14 per person),

Texas, and New York were in the bottom ten of all 50 states.[21] Although no data

suggests that Wyoming or North Dakota were facing increased threats during this period,

the SHSGP minimum distribution formula required this counterintuitive imbalance.

On top of the per capita divide, backwater locales won hollow victories with

windfalls of grant money thanks to Congress favoring political calculations over risk.

Examples of lawmakers spreading the wealth persist: Christian County, Kentucky

(population 100,000) received nearly $40,000 worth of extraneous equipment to respond

to a chemical, biological, or radiological emergency; nearly $1 million for the

Massachusetts Steamship Authority; and a $58,000 search-and-rescue vehicle for

Colchester, Vermont (population 18,000).[22] Despite reluctantly accepting these items,

localities generally have accepted superfluous aid, perhaps to insulate themselves from

criticism in the event of an unforeseen emergency.

Unfortunately, this behavior provided positive reinforcement for elected officials,

who continued the trend for several years. Professor Anne Khademian agreed, saying in

2004 that "money continues to be spent without regard to a broad national strategy for

preparedness or with much attentiveness to the particular needs of high-risk areas."[23]

Former DHS Official Matt A. Mayer identified the persisting issue in 2010, and called for

an end to sending money to low-risk areas saying, "It's time Congress ended the pork

barrel nature of the homeland security grants. Lawmakers should require DHS to conduct

a comprehensive capabilities assessment, and should focus future funds to those 30 or so

---

[21] Ibid.

[22] O'Beirne.

[23] Donald F. Kettl,"The Deparment of Homeland Security's First Year," *The Century Foundation*, http://tcf.org/publications/2004/3/pb451 (accessed November 28, 2012).

states and cities where the vulnerabilities are many and the consequences of a terrorist attack are high."[24] This trend shows no signs of abating as Senator Coburn's 2012 report states, "an examination of the last 10 years of the program raises questions about the role of political influence, lobbying and pork barrel spending in deciding where homeland security dollars have been spent."[25]

Though UASI grants were initially designed to favor risk-based factors, they too were not immune to wasteful allocation. First allocating $96 million to New York, Washington, DC, Los Angeles, Seattle, Chicago, San Francisco, and Houston, UASI would swell to another $506 million for a total of 30 eligible cities in 2003.[26] Inertia overcame the noble and focused start to the UASI, growing to $832 million for more than 64 urban areas in FY2010.[27] Adding to the negative trend here was the division between Tier I and Tier II UASI grants; Tier I grantees like New York and Washington received money based on threats while Tier II recipients lacked the same justification, according to the Government Accountability Office.[28] Thanks to sloppy allocation, built on a questionable grants development process, the Department of Homeland Security not only limited its ability to augment nationwide counterterrorism capacity, but also hurt its image and clout.

Grants Administration

Reviewing the mechanisms for moving money to state and local governments reveals a cumbersome system mired by an overriding attempt at accountability. While

---

[24] Matt A. Mayer, "Pork Payoffs in Homeland Security Jeopardize Americans," The Heritage Foundation, http://www.heritage.org/research/commentary/2010/01/pork-payoffs-in-homeland-security-jeopardize-americans (accessed February 12, 2013).
[25] Coburn, 14.
[26] Lakoff and Klinenberg, 509-510.
[27] Rittgers.
[28] Ibid.

accountability is vital, it must be reasoned and complement larger CT goals. Between

2001 and 2004, Washington identified more than $23 billion for state and local

counterterrorism efforts, but roughly a third of that money stalled in the pipeline because

of complex administration.[29] The sluggish distribution of nearly $8 billion dollars speaks

to the structural flaws in the DHS grants process. Ambassador Matthew Brzezinski

writes:

> …even monies already earmarked for counterterror expenditures were
> getting snared in red tape and not making it out of federal coffers. The
> port of Charleston, for instance, was awarded a $3.7 million grant from
> DHS that includes $2 million designated for the purchase of a helicopter
> for the Charleston County Sheriff's Department. But according to the
> September 9, 2003, edition of the *Washington Post*, DHS later informed
> county officials that they couldn't buy a chopper, due to some clerical
> snafu, and that therefore the port of Charleston couldn't spend the $2
> million allotted to it.[30]

Brzezinski's anecdote is just one of many attributed to the onerous grants process. States

and localities faced mountains of paperwork, consisting of unfamiliar forms that required

a shift of focus away from operations and towards administrative duties.[31] Difficulties in

grants administration develop, in part, from the one-sided development process. Had

state or local governments been partners in developing grant programs, the likely result is

a user-friendly process to aid the flow of funds. Without an institutional structure able to

analyze and adapt problem sets, grants were totally undermined as highlighted in the case

above. Underscoring these concerns, the U.S. Conference of Mayors said in January

---

[29] Sibley Fleming, "Where Did the Buck Stop?" *American City & County* 118, no. 8 (July 2004): 41.

[30] Matthew Brzezinski, *Fortress America: On the Front Lines of Homeland Security – An Inside Look at the Coming Surveillance State,* (New York, NY: Bantam Books, 2004), 236.

[31] Anonymous, "Homeland Security has $4 Billion in Police Grants for those who Learn Rules," *Crime Control Digest* 37, no. 25 (June 27, 2003): 1.

2004 that "in a survey of 215 major cities, 90 percent reported they had not received any funding from the biggest program for first responders."[32]

Complicating the process for entities below the state level – cities, counties, and others – is a federal requirement that most federal funds pass through state capitals first, the result of which is "cities and counties are always concerned that the state is siphoning off the resources."[33] Under the rules for many federal grant programs, local governments are required to spend first and get reimbursed only after some 20 percent of grant money may be kept by state officials for their administration costs.[34] In this respect, federal grants have the potential to become big business for state intermediaries, taking a percentage of all local "wins" much like a plaintiff's attorney does for cash verdicts.

Further diluting the impact of big-figure grants, "nearly half of the states determined that the county was the local level. In those cases, money was distributed to the counties, but not to the cities where the first responders were."[35] For programs designed to get speedy assistance to those most in need, DHS grants contained tripwires that prevented true federal assistance based on need. The Task Force on Homeland Security Funding identified five problem areas with grant administration: a failure to consider risk-based funding or offer overtime compensation; the reimbursement requirement; communication failures in the process; and the burdensome workload of the grant system on overwhelmed state and local governments.[36]

---

[32] Donald F. Kettl, "Unconnected Dots," *Governing* 17, no. 7 (April 2004): 14.
[33] Charles R. Wise and Rania Nader, "Organizing the Federal System for Homeland Security: Problems, Issues, and Dilemmas," Special Issue. *Public Administration Review* 62 (September 2002): 49.
[34] Kettl, "Unconnected Dots," 14.
[35] Ibid.
[36] Ibid.

Grants Assessment & Accountability

Evaluating the effectiveness of grant money helps justify funding and reduce waste. Unfortunately, developing performance metrics for massive spending programs – particularly those designed to prevent and respond to terrorism – raise further challenges. It is not always easy to see the value of preventative grant money. Short of connecting a failed plot to a piece of equipment purchased with federal dollars, the justification for DHS grants programs risks going unnoticed. A recent study notes that to justify the rapid increase in homeland security funding "[the government] would have to deter, prevent, foil, or protect against 1,667 otherwise successful [attempted Times Square car bomb] type attacks per year, or more than four per day."[37] Though there is little doubt that state and local governments require federal assistance to fight terrorism, it cannot come as a blank check without mechanisms to judge implementation.

The risk becomes that performance metrics transform into bureaucratic tourniquets that slow the flow of aid because they are blind to feedback from grantees. In the earliest grant programs, states were required to submit lists of line-item expenses from grants, an arduous requirement that hardly illustrated preparedness.[38] Getting to the root cause of the problem, the Council on Foreign Relations questioned the value of homeland security grants:

> The overall effectiveness of federal funding has been further diluted by the lack of a process to determine the most critical needs of the emergency

---

[37] Rittgers.

[38] U.S. Government Accountability Office (GAO), *Homeland Security: Management of First Responder Grant Programs and Efforts to Improve Accountability Continue to Evolve*, by William O. Jenkins, Jr., GAO Director, Homeland Security and Justice (Washington, DC: Government Printing Office, 2005), 3.

responder community in order to achieve the greatest return on investments.[39]

Logically, with no baseline for preparedness, developing metrics to analyze preparedness is a moot point. By 2005, the federal government agreed as DHS moved to results-based reporting to gauge the impact of state spending on preparedness.[40] As DHS released guidance in 2006 that amounted to a "baseline for measuring preparedness," Homeland Security Secretary Chertoff shifted the burden to the states, calling for them to develop performance indicators to boost accountability.[41] While states lacked administrative staff to manage grants applications, the DHS suggestion that fifty states develop their own performance indicators to help justify funding is laughable. The lack of manpower aside, if every state created their own metrics, a national analysis of the data would be critically flawed.

Plagued by rushed development, implementation, and evaluation, the flaws in DHS grants threaten to undermine their usefulness. Ultimately, rushed grants amounted to comforting headlines that the federal government was helping, but without a system to track the value of federal handouts, both the donors and the recipients were disadvantaged. This analysis yields little evidence that federal grants equal better domestic counterterrorism capabilities, but there may be a chance for reform. Coming as a response to the politically-driven SHSGP's all-inclusive and wasteful mechanism, the UASI's narrow focus and risk-based motivations offered a positive example for DHS grant programs. Further chances to draw best practices from the UASI decreased in 2012

[39] Warren Rudman, *Emergency Responders: Drastically Underfunded, Dangerously Unprepared: Report of an Independent Task Force Sponsored by the Council on Foreign Relations,* (New York, NY: Council on Foreign Relations Press, 2003), 9-10.
[40] U.S. Government Accountability Office, 3.
[41] U.S. Department of Homeland Security, *Keynote Address by Secretary of Homeland Security Michael Chertoff to the 2006 Grants & Training National Conference, by Michael Chertoff, Secretary of Homeland Security*, Government Printing Office (Washington, DC, 2006).

when the Obama Administration "proposed to consolidate 16 state and local grant programs overseen by the Federal Emergency Management Agency into the National Preparedness Grant Program (NPGP)." The implications of introducing yet another sweeping change to the DHS grant program are likely to stifle the progress existing reforms.

In testimony before Congress in April 2012, Deputy Commissioner Richard Daddario of New York City Police Department urged Congress to maintain the UASI after President Obama's FY2013 budget proposed consolidating UASI with many other grant programs.[42] The change risks a loss of momentum and the key attributes that made the program effective: risk-based funding, regional considerations, and a functioning governance framework.[43] Despite a seemingly unchanged threat, the decision to eliminate UASI and fold it into a larger program shows the repercussions of political decisions on state and local partners hungry for federal funds. More than a decade after 9/11, when strategy and policy reflected rushed reaction, the continuing problem cannot be attributed to haste, but rather deeper failings in a strategy beholden to political pressure.

Changes to the grant process at all stages could produce a system that accomplishes multiple goals: sharing counterterrorism responsibilities with locals that have expertise and expansive networks; empowering states with much-needed resources; and protecting taxpayers from attacks while also preventing fraud, waste, and abuse. The

---

[42] House Committee on Homeland Security, Subcommittee on Emergency Preparedness, Response, and Communication, *Homeland Security Grants Oversight: Testimony of Richard Daddario*, Government Printing Office (Washington, DC, 2012), 2.
[43] Ibid.

next section of this case study will explore another vehicle for federal aid that overlaps with grants, but focuses more on information sharing: the fusion center approach.

DHS Fusion Centers

Directly addressing information sharing deficiencies, state and local governments across the United States created or expanded more than 70 fusion centers since 2003, partly supported by federal funds.[44] The growth of fusion centers under both the Bush and Obama administrations signaled continued interest in bridging the gap between federal and state and local partners, but conclusive data about the value of these centers remains elusive. This discussion will highlight how the innovative idea of the fusion center became derailed early in its development. Studying the genesis of these fusion centers, their poor management under federal stewardship, and their perceived underwhelming results to date, highlights the difficulties of managing homeland security from Washington.

Growing Fusion Centers: A State and Local Initiative Hijacked

The Los Angeles County Terrorism Early Warning Center (LACTEW) that opened in 1996 is considered the forerunner to the network of fusion centers that developed after 9/11.[45] The federal government defines a fusion center as a "collaborative effort of two or more agencies that provide resources, expertise, and information to the center with goal of maximizing their ability to detect, prevent,

---

[44] Senate Committee on Homeland Security and Governmental Affairs, Senate Permanent Subcommittee on Investigations, *Federal Support for and Inolvement in State and Local Fusion Centers*, Majority and Minority Staff Report, Government Printing Office (Washington, DC, 2012), 1.

[45] Torin Monahan, "The Future of Security? Surveillance Operations at Homeland Security Fusion Centers," *Social Justice* 37, no. 2-3 (2010-2011): 85.

investigate, and respond to criminal and terrorist activity."[46] A central characteristic of most fusion centers is that they reside within state and local police departments.[47] Fusion centers have enjoyed deep federal support in terms of funding and personnel, but they began like the LACTEW with the needs of localities in mind. Leading a homeland security working group in 2004, then Massachusetts Governor Mitt Romney explained that "to protect America against terrorists, state and local agencies, as well as private businesses, need to gather intelligence themselves and not just rely on intelligence gathered by the federal government.[48]

In its second year as a cabinet department, it is interesting that this idea did not originate with DHS even though DHS offered substantial support and attention. Seizing on popular concept, the Departments of Justice and Homeland Security created guidance documents to streamline and standardize fusion centers throughout the country. These agencies called the fusion center model "an effective and efficient mechanism to exchange information and intelligence, maximize resources, streamline operations, and improve the ability to fight crime and terrorism…"[49] Over the course of several years, the federal government poured around $1.4 billion in funding to fusion centers.[50] Clamoring for aid and bringing a bottom-up model to the table, homeland security professionals in states and cities found willing donors in Washington, but they soon found support came with conditions.

---

[46] U.S. Department of Justice, Bureau of Justice Assistance, *Fusion Center Guidelines: Developing and Sharing Information and Intelligence in a New Era*, Office of Justice Programs, Government Printing Office (Washington, DC, 2006), 2.

[47] Torin Monahan and Neal A. Palmer, "The Emerging Politics of DHS Fusion Centers," *Security Dialogue* 40, no. 6 (December 2009): 619.

[48] Pam Belluck, "States and Cities Must Hunt Terror Plots, Governor Says," *The New York Times*, December 15, 2004.

[49] U.S. Department of Justice, Bureau of Justice Assistance, 2.

[50] Robert O'Harrow Jr., "DHS 'Fusion Centers' Portrayed as Pools of Ineptitude, Civil Liberties Intrusions," *The Washington Post*, October 2, 2012.

Whereas state and local governments sought better information about threats in their communities, DHS saw fusion centers primarily as a force multiplier to support limited federal resources. A report by the Senate Permanent Subcommittee on Investigations found:

> In 2006, the Department's intelligence chief penned a master plan for how DHS should use fusion centers to contribute to the U.S. intelligence community. "Harnessing domestic information is the unique DHS contribution to the national-level mission to protect the Homeland," wrote Charles Allen, then Under Secretary for Intelligence and Analysis, in the Department's strategy for systematic engagement with fusion centers. "We need the capability to routinely harvest information and finished intelligence in a timely manner from State and Local sources.[51]

Rather than talking about two-way information sharing or building capacity in partners, DHS looked to take advantage of the fusion center network to supplement its own dearth of intelligence. The progression of this concept from matching federal resources and local expertise to the one-sided data-mining operation described above demonstrates the warped relationship between Washington and its partners.

On the surface, an initiative developed by local actors, housed in their departments, and receiving federal aid without micromanagement, is an ideal arrangement. With deepening federal involvement, though, came increased pressure for results and a temptation to hijack the fusion center mission. Conflicting agendas threaten results, and with opposing perspectives, the success of fusion centers remains stymied. After the initial excitement over an infusion of federal funding, there was a notable shift in sentiment when funding came with greater constraints. Increasingly, "state and local governments see too heavy an emphasis on national issues that are not obvious threats to every locality, and states argue that money awarded to fusion centers could be used more

---

[51] Senate Committee on Homeland Security and Governmental Affairs, 26.

effectively if states had more say in the allocation process."[52] As fusion centers move

from a concept championed by state and local officials to a superficial accomplishment

touted by DHS to justify past expenditures, their relevance is endangered. An approach

that harnessing existing state and local capabilities and opinion will undoubtedly perform

better than a failing idea promulgated from Washington.

Mismanagement Impedes Information Sharing

Once fusion centers morphed from an attempt "to work around the problem of

FBI policies that precluded sharing information with local and state agencies"[53] into a

program championed by the Department of Homeland Security, state and local actors

should have reacted with skepticism. A valiant effort to sidestep government

bureaucracy became a signature program of the standard-bearer for that bureaucracy,

which routinely ranks at the bottom of employee satisfaction surveys amidst other

criticisms.[54] Rather than simply providing the centers with information, as originally

intended, DHS approached the relationship by infusing its own bureaucratic baggage.

The Congressional Research Service (CRS) found it critical to "ensure that the centers

retain their state and local-level identity and support from those communities."[55]

Reshaping individual fusion centers in the image of a mini-federal bureaucracy

contradicts not only the spirit of their founding, but also marginalizes the input of state

and local partners. The CRS acknowledged this challenge:

---

[52] Monahan and Palmer, 622.

[53] Rittgers.

[54] Partnership for Public Service, "The Best Places to Work in the Federal Government," Partnership for Public Service, http://www.bestplacestowork.org/BPTW/rankings/detail/HS00 (accessed December 12, 2012).

[55] Congressional Research Service, *Fusion Centers: Issues and Options for Congress, by John Rollins, Congressional Research Service, January 18, 2008* (Washington, DC: Government Printing Office, 2008), 37.

> Part of the challenge from the federal perspective has been how to guide, but not dictate to, the "owners and operators" of these largely state-established entities prior to the provision of any federal financial support. And, once federal financial and human resources support was provided, how to coordinate and target these resources for maximum overall return on investment.[56]

As the new DHS sought to widen its influence and grow its role within a crowded field dominated by the FBI, it looked to mold the centers in its own image, a troubling development. Finding the balance between federal support and coordination without dictating policy is common theme in the counterterrorism debate. Losing that balance risks undermining programs with potential, like fusion centers, and erecting another barrier to information sharing.

Preliminary Results Are Poor

Fusion centers are different things to different organizations, an inherent flaw that clouds measuring their success. For some lawmakers, the centers are merely depositories of federal funding that can be championed as successes to constituents and build legacies. To state and local officials, they may grant access to federal officials or information previously lost in layers of bureaucracy, at best. And for leaders at the Department of Homeland Security, fusion centers could signal the very justification for survival of their mammoth agency. Depending on which of these three lenses one looks, the performance of fusion centers remains debatable. Since each of these perspectives has limits standing alone, exploring the three comparatively sketches the best performance picture available for fusion centers to date.

An October 2012 Senate investigation provides an in-depth and scathing account of fusion center performance to date; consequently, claims of the centers as "pools of

---

[56] Ibid.

ineptitude, waste, and civil liberties intrusions" will undoubtedly draw greater oversight for the Department of Homeland Security.[57] The 141-page report made nine major recommendations to rehabilitate DHS support for fusion centers, which range from designing performance metrics to improving training for federal employees assigned to the centers.[58] Three key problems identified at fusion centers forecast dangerous trends for DHS. Misuse of federal funds, poor intelligence reporting, and improper information handling all undermine the mission of these centers while abrogating information sharing gains.[59]

Similar to earlier discussions about the faults in the overall grants process, fusion center funding comes from the same SHSGP fund, rife with its own problems.[60] Although purchases like "dozens of flat-screen TVs" or SUVs given away to other local partners were allowed under grant rules, they are hard to justify in the face of critical information technology needs going unfunded.[61] The issue then returns to states or localities spending funds rather than lose them, but neither of these spending examples facilitates improved information sharing, an overarching fusion center goal.

The Senate committee examined fusion center intelligence reporting between April 1, 2009 and April 30, 2010 finding "no reporting which uncovered a terrorist threat, nor could it identify a contribution such center reporting made to disrupt an active terrorist plot."[62] Though unimpressive statistic, this finding does not obviate the usefulness of fusion centers because the absence of threat detection does not correspond

---

[57] O'Harrow.
[58] Senate Committee on Homeland Security and Governmental Affairs, 106-107.
[59] Ibid., 1-4.
[60] Ben Bain, "Funding Worries Fusion Center Officials," *Federal Computer Week*, April 21, 2008.
[61] Senate Committee on Homeland Security and Governmental Affairs, 3.
[62] Ibid., 2.

to greater insecurity. A counterargument is that simply keeping an open dialogue, building relationships, and looking at problems from all levels of government is required to overcome the stratified U.S. CT system. While it is difficult to pinpoint where a future terrorist plot is disrupted, but that point should not insulate fusion centers from all scrutiny.

Nearly one-third of all fusion center intelligence reports examined "were never published for use within DHS and by other members of the intelligence community, often because they lacked any useful information, or potentially violated Department guidelines meant to protect Americans' civil liberties or Privacy Act protections."[63] Emphasizing the concerns about misuse of resources and improper information sharing, the Senate report recommended that "DHS should strengthen its protections to prevent DHS personnel from improperly collecting and retaining intelligence on Constitutionally protected activity.[64] As noted in other sections of this paper, running afoul of Congress with perceived or actual domestic intelligence activities generally results in restricted powers for agencies and risks undoing advances in information sharing since 9/11. For fusion centers to be successful, DHS needs to implement better internal controls rather than face newer and more stringent legislation that would ultimately slow information flow to state and local partners.

Among the most disconcerting findings of the Senate investigation is conflicting messaging from DHS. The report details the dichotomy between positive public comments about the usefulness of fusion centers and "internal reviews and non-public assessments [that] highlighted problems at the centers and dysfunction in DHS's own

---

[63] Ibid., 2.
[64] Ibid., 107.

operations."[65] Such a trend undercuts the credibility of DHS while also preventing

honest self-assessment and improvement.

Throughout the Department of Homeland Security's short history, critics have

lined up to challenge its methods and its purpose, so it is no surprise that DHS maintains

a strong public relations effort to reassure the American people and highlight the

agency's strengths. The surprise comes in what DHS chooses to count as successes,

particularly relative to fusion centers. On the DHS public webpage, following a link to

"Fusion Center Successes," one finds the following press release, entitled "Fusion Center

Enables a Teen Runaway to Return Home Safely:

> In May 2012, a teenager ran away from their home in Pennsylvania.
> Through further investigation, local officers were able to determine that
> the juvenile had been in communication with an individual in Virginia for
> an extended period of time. Upon discovering this information, the local
> officers were put in contact with the Virginia Fusion Center (VFC).
> Taking action, a VFC analyst promptly provided this information to the
> Virginia State Police, who were able to locate the juvenile. This example
> of timely information sharing enabled the juvenile to safely return home.[66]

No doubt a feel-good story, it is unclear why DHS is claiming this incident as a success,

particularly absent a nexus to terrorism and only a marginal link to information sharing.

It is likely a local police officer could liaise with the Virginia State Police without DHS

getting involved. Understandably, fusion centers will serve more than one role, and the

fact that many have grown beyond the mandate of counterterrorism is a natural and

positive evolution. DHS claiming this routine law enforcement process – that does not

even involve a crime – hints that there are few substantive successes to promote.

Furthermore, in its own fact sheet on fusion centers, DHS makes only fleeting references

---

[65] Ibid., 4.
[66] U.S. Department of Homeland Security, "Fusion Center Success Stories," U.S. Department of Homeland Security, http://www.dhs.gov/fusion-center-success-stories (accessed December 13, 2012).

to crime prevention and focuses mainly on counterterrorism and information sharing missions.[67] In reviewing the 23 cases listed on this same webpage, less than one quarter have a nexus to terrorism.[68]

The popularity of fusion centers – there are more centers than states – shows that state and local officials place high importance on them. By creating and hosting the majority of these centers, dedicating personnel to them, and lobbying for additional funds in support of them, state and local players have spoken. Although plenty of evidence details the assorted challenges of fusion centers, from questions over theoretical and practical missions to funding and management, the model is not beyond recovery. Support for the principle that the federal officials needed to integrate into state and local structures while sharing information was unthinkable prior to 9/11, so the creation of these fusion centers alone is promising. The key to increased and sustained success for this model must be federal involvement and support for fusion centers that falls short of dominance.

DHS faces challenges accomplishing a nebulous mission with a conglomeration of organizations with a wide range of missions and cultures. Within its vast responsibilities, DHS grant programs and fusion centers hold the greatest potential for harnessing state and local contributions to national counterterrorism efforts. In the rush to help state and local partners in the wake of 9/11, DHS faltered in these two efforts. Uneven Congressional oversight has complicated efforts to reform these two essential

---

[67] U.S. Department of Homeland Security, "National Network of Fusion Center Fact Sheet," U.S. Department of Homeland Security, http://www.dhs.gov/national-network-fusion-centers-fact-sheet (accessed December 13, 2012).
[68] Ibid.

vehicles for incorporating state and local partners responsibly. Further changes are

underway at the time of this writing, but real improvements to DHS are yet to be realized.

CHAPTER 6: THE JOINT TERRORISM TASK FORCE: A JOINT APPROACH

The JTTF: From Buzzword to Standard-Bearer

After studying top-down and bottom-up approaches to U.S. counterterrorism

policy, the next logical subject to review is one that blends aspects of both. This chapter

explores the validity of the Joint Terrorism Task Force (JTTF) as a joint approach.

Existing prior to 9/11, but growing in number and notoriety in the years since, the JTTF

model "was founded on the belief that interagency cooperation is essential to effectively

tackle terrorism because the complex crime of terrorism cuts across agency lines and

must transcend agency rivalries."[1]

This analysis begins with a brief history of the JTTF and its transformation in the

post 9/11 Era followed by a survey of how "joint" the concept really is. With perspective

about its history and organization, the focus moves to judgments of the JTTF by key

players: state and local partners, the Congress, and the executive branch. Distilling the

positive and negative JTTF trends leads to the essential task of capturing lessons learned.

The case study concludes with a discussion of adapting the model beyond major

metropolitan areas.

The NYPD and FBI Establish the JTTF

In 1980, the NYPD and FBI established the first Joint Terrorism Task Force in

response to threats from ethnic-nationalist groups in New York.[2] Drawing on local

expertise of NYPD detectives and the global reach of the FBI, the JTTF integrated and

---

[1] Mary Jo White, "Prosecuting Terrorism in New York," *Middle East Quarterly* 8, no. 2 (Spring 2001): 11.

[2] Mathieu Deflem, "Joint Terrorism Task Forces," In *Counterterrorism: From the Cold War to the War on Terror, Volume 1* (Santa Barbara, CA: Praeger, 2012), 423.

harnessed diversity to fight international terrorists in the city.[3] Long before the term

terrorism entered daily use in the United States, New York City served as the test case for

this pioneering counterterrorism effort. The creation of a standing counterterrorism task

force, as opposed to one formed in response to a pattern of threats, reinforces two ideas.

First, New York's outlier status historically exposed it to unique risk while facilitating

innovative solutions as much as it does today. Second, federal leadership acknowledged

the value of combining federal, state, and local efforts to maximize resources, provide

sophisticated investigative resources, and link with other U.S. government efforts

worldwide.[4] In taking this early step to elevate the involvement of local partners, the first

JTTF's birth marked the first stage in U.S. counterterrorism evolution. Ultimately,

circumstances did not dictate the diffusion of the JTTF model beyond New York until

terrorism came to the forefront of national life some two decades later.

From One, Many: the JTTF Expands

Attracting widespread acclaim and facing limited criticism, the JTTF expanded its

reach to 103 cities, 71 of those since 9/11, and is comprised of more than 4,400

individuals hailing from approximately 650 agencies.[5] The FBI website promotes the

benefits of this model, explaining that JTTFs:

> …provide one-stop shopping for information regarding terrorist activities.
> They enable a shared intelligence base across many agencies. They create
> familiarity among investigators and managers before a crisis. And
> perhaps most importantly, they pool talents, skills, and knowledge from
> across the law enforcement and intelligence communities into a single
> team that responds together.[6]

---

[3] Robert A. Martin, "The Joint Terrorism Task Force: A Concept that Works," *FBI Law Enforcement Bulletin* 68, no. 3 (March 1999): 24.
[4] Ibid., 4.
[5] Federal Bureau of Investigation, "Joint Terrorism Task Forces," Federal Bureau of Investigation, http://www.fbi.gov/about-us/investigate/terrorism/terrorism_jttfs (accessed December 14, 2012).
[6] Ibid.

A critical component to the success of the JTTF is the sense of team and shared goals. An overriding focus of interdicting terrorists before attacks means task force members set aside parochial behaviors in favor of a common approach. Some second order effects are improved intelligence sharing and cross-agency relationships that bolster trust between federal and local officials.

A useful tool for select cities prior to September 11, 2001 the JTTF transformed into a panacea for some in the wake of the devastating attacks. Although primarily concerned with proactive counterterrorism investigations, these secondary gains from JTTF expansion continue to reinforce the program's popularity. The FBI, for one, considers the JTTFs "the nation's front line on terrorism" and has increased the number of top secret security clearances issued to local law enforcement on JTTFs "from 125 to 878 between 2007 and 2009."[7] Whereas restrictions on security clearances for local officials and a background investigation bottleneck were often cited complaints in the early 2000s, this course correction demonstrates the will and capacity of the FBI to share more.

Acknowledging the explosive growth in JTTFs post 9/11, the FBI created the National JTTF "to FBI formed the NJTTF to coordinate the flow of information on threats and leads between the FBI headquarters and the JTTFs and to function as the "hub" of support for the JTTFs throughout the United States."[8] Headquartered in

---

[7] Congressional Research Service, *The Federal Bureau of Investigation and Terrorism Investigations, by the Congressional Research Service, December 28, 2011* (Washington, DC: Government Printing Office, 2011), 14.

[8] U.S. Department of Justice, Office of the Inspector General, *The Department of Justice's Terrorism Task Forces*, Evaluation and Inspections Division, Government Printing Office (Washington, DC, 2005), 21.

Washington, the NJTTF is a natural extension of the program with growth in order to ensure cohesiveness.

Determining "Jointness" on the JTTF

Seeking the best model for state and local law enforcement to support national counterterrorism efforts necessitates an analysis of the "joint" nature of the Joint Terrorism Task Force. An in-depth review of the JTTF structure and processes reveals that a positive reputation and terrorism prevention successes do not necessarily stem from equal partnerships between the federal government and its state and local counterparts. A typical JTTF is housed in an FBI Field Office and managed by an FBI Supervisory Special Agent.[9] JTTF members "are recruited from other agencies, yet work in function of FBI objectives" creating a force-multiplier for the FBI.[10] Initially, JTTF detailees were prohibited from debriefing home agencies about JTTF investigations in many cases, but this restriction has been mitigated in recent years.[11]

Rather than an equal partnership, this snapshot of the model portrays an alternative FBI field office unit comprised of traditional FBI agents and detailees deputized to assist the pursuit of FBI objectives. It does not describe an open forum where state or local law enforcement share management of investigative priorities, though it is conceivable that their voices are heard. Although FBI goals of preventing terrorism and prosecuting offenders also benefit state, local, and other federal law enforcement, FBI leadership undoubtedly favors FBI culture, structure, and processes. A Customs and Border Protection Officer or a New York State Trooper serving on the

---

[9] Ibid., 15.
[10] Deflem, 424.
[11] U.S. Department of Justice, Community Oriented Policing Services, *Protecting Your Community from Terrorism: Strategies for Local Law Enforcement, Volume 1: Local-Federal Partnerships*, Police Executive Research Forum, Government Printing Office (Washington, DC, 2003), 9.

Buffalo JTTF do not necessarily influence what investigations are pursued or through what means. This begs the question of whether the JTTF is a conduit for improving the participation of local law enforcement, or if is merely a clever tool to increase FBI manpower without assuming massive costs.

Drawing larger lessons from a collection of JTTFs across the country proves challenging because JTTF efforts have not always been unified. The 9/11 Commission Report noted that JTTFs were useful, but cautioned that "[t]hey set priorities in accordance with regional and field office concerns."[12] Citing lapses in the case of the Fort Hood shootings, a 2011 U.S. Senate report notes:

> In the Hasan case, two JTTFs (each located in a different field office) disputed the significance of Hasan's communications with the Suspected Terrorist and how vigorously he should be investigated…Two key headquarters units – the Counterterrorism Division, the 'National JTTF' (which was created specifically to be the hub among JTTFs), and the Directorate of Intelligence were not made aware of the dispute.[13]

Years after a major organization and efforts to avoid too much autonomy among field offices across the country, this case highlights that agency culture has not kept pace with bureaucratic reorganization and that no two JTTFs are necessarily the same. The Senate report goes on to state that "despite the more assertive role that FBI headquarters now plays, especially since 9/11 in what historically has been a decentralized organization, field offices still prize and protect their autonomy from headquarters."[14]

Independence and autonomy, as seen in the NYPD case study, can prove valuable as powerful innovators. The experience to experiment at one JTTF may develop a best

---

[12] National Commission on Terrorist Attacks Upon the United States, *Final Report of the National Commission on Terrorist Attacks Upon the United States*, Government Printing Office (Washington, DC, 2004), 82.
[13] Senate Committee on Homeland Security and Governmental Affairs, *A Ticking Time Bomb: Counterterrorism Lessons from the U.S. Government's Failure to Prevent the Fort Hood Attack*, Government Printing Office (Washington, DC, 2011), 10.
[14] Ibid.

practice to be shared by FBI headquarters and replicated throughout the country. The

Heart of America (HOA) JTTF in Kansas City, Missouri features a Counterterrorism

Executive Board (CEB) that employs a unique format to improve partnership between the

FBI and its partners.[15] The CEB ensures officials from all agencies receive threat

briefings and "are given the opportunity to provide operational input on how those threats

could be addressed," a feature that involves officials from all levels of government "in

the operations decisions of select JTTF investigation initiatives, rather than making them

merely the passive recipients of intelligence information.[16] Going a step further, the CEB

even includes issue-specific subject matter experts like medical professionals and

representatives of other government agencies that may not necessarily contribute

investigators to the JTTF.[17] This format emphasizes inclusiveness and allows for shared

decision-making, which promotes unique approaches to counterterrorism by addressing

complex problems outside of standard bureaucratic processes and structures. A welcome

addition to the JTTF model, the HOA JTTF's Counterterrorism Executive Board

demonstrates the value of growing and testing concepts in the field vice relying on

directives issued from Washington. To ensure that the CEB approach is not isolated to

the personal flexibility of the FBI's Special Agent in Charge in Kansas City, headquarters

should play a role identifying best practices and institutionalizing them for maximum

effect.

---

[15] U.S. Department of Justice, Community Oriented Policing Services, 39.
[16] Ibid.
[17] Ibid.

The JTTF: A State & Local Perspective

State and local governments have generally supported the JTTF concept from its inception to its rapid growth with only minor examples of resistance. This trend is evident in the scale of participation alone: more than 600 state and local agencies participate in over 100 JTTFs nationwide.[18] However, appreciation for the model does not translate into blind support for its management. The New York City Police Department's presence on a JTTF for more than 30 years illustrates not only the successes of the model, but also its flaws. During the late 1980s and early 1990s, the FBI withheld information from NYPD JTTF members and created an information stovepipe that saw the NYPD duplicating efforts of existing FBI investigations.[19] Years later, the NYPD reversed this negative trend by "packing scores more NYPD detectives into the JTTF and bringing them under [the NYPD's] direct supervision."[20] In its current form, New York's political and law enforcement leadership firmly support JTTF efforts, but still maintain an independent streak thanks to the NYPD's Intelligence Division and Counter-Terrorism Bureau, signaling New York's efforts to minimize risk if its partnership suffers.

Lacking the exceptionalism of the NYPD, other local law enforcement organizations have navigated concerns about the JTTF differently. Portland, Oregon became the only city to ever withdraw from a JTTF in 2005 over worries that the JTTF illegitimately targeted the city's Muslims and concern that Portland could not sufficiently

---

[18] Federal Bureau of Investigation, "Joint Terrorism Task Forces."
[19] Christopher Dickey, *Securing The City: Inside America's Best Counterterror Force – The NYPD* (New York, NY: Simon & Schuster, 2009), 58-59.
[20] Ibid., 71.

monitor its officers on the task force.[21] Civil libertarians have also pressured local

leaders in San Francisco, California and Dearborn, Michigan to consider potential

drawbacks of JTTF support. Highlighting the concerns, the same Senate panel that

faulted the JTTF on the Hasan investigation found "that JTTFs are not fulfilling the FBI's

vision of being interagency information-sharing and operational coordination

mechanisms but rather may merely be appendages of the FBI."[22] These two themes are

crucial in assessing the JTTF as a means for better inclusivity and partnership with state

and local law enforcement.

While leadership in Dearborn, among other cities, bristled at Department of

Justice requests to interview visa holders of Middle Eastern descent after 9/11, the city

maintained its ties to the JTTF because of the benefit to the city.[23] Dearborn's police

officers assisted and accompanied federal agents in these interviews, but refused to

conduct them on behalf of the federal government.[24] Professor David Thacher from the

University of Michigan's Gerald Ford School of Public Policy explains why Dearborn

favors continued involvement with the JTTF in spite of substantive reservations:

> ...one reason is the sense of occupational purpose and national duty that
> played a role in other offender search activities, such as the Justice
> Department interviews. But involvement with the JTTF also has direct
> benefits to the city, by both enhancing its capacity for community
> protection and-paradoxically-minimizing its offender search
> responsibilities.[25]

---

[21] Kris Erickson, John Carr, and Steve Herbert, "The Scales of Justice: Federal-Local Tensions in the War on Terror," In *Uniform Behavior: Police Localism and National Politics* (Gordonsville, VA: Palgrave Macmillan, 2006), 231.

[22] Senate Committee on Homeland Security and Governmental Affairs, 4.

[23] David Thacher, "The Local Role in Homeland Security," *Law & Society Review* 39, no. 3 (September 2005): 658.

[24] Ibid., 659.

[25] Ibid., 666.

For Thacher, cities too can use a JTTF as a force-multiplier much as the FBI do. In this case, city law enforcement assists on an as-needed basis, and are otherwise free to pursue conventional police work, but this arrangement is dependent on the city's willingness to leave counterterrorism operations to the federal government; consequently, local leaders stay abreast of developments, but do not shape policy.

Returning to the Portland example, despite leaving the JTTF in 2005, the city rejoined the body in 2011, but not without concessions. After being surprised by the FBI's public announcement of an arrest in connection with a major terrorist investigation in Portland, the city's mayor pursued a return to the JTTF.[26] Portland's shift came only after securing special considerations that held its officers to more restrictive Oregon state law – a stipulation intended to better protect civil liberties – and required them to consult with the city attorney when questions arise.[27]

Congressional Response to the JTTF Approach

As referenced earlier in this case study, a 2011 Senate report investigating the Fort Hood shooting criticized the JTTF model on a number of fronts, but sought JTTF improvement vice elimination, a sign of its larger support for the model. The 2009 case of Najibullah Zazi, accused of receiving bomb-making instructions in Pakistan and planning an attack in New York City is one example of JTTF success noted by lawmakers.[28] The Senate lauded JTTF efforts that "unraveled and prevented a massive attack on the New York City subway system," citing its "coordination across federal,

---

[26] William Yardley, "Portland, Ore., Votes to Rejoin Task Force after Terrorism Scare," *The New York Times*, April 30, 2011.

[27] Ibid.

[28] Federal Bureau of Investigation, "New York Terror Case: Indictment Announced," Federal Bureau of Investigation, http://www.fbi.gov/news/stories/2009/september/zazi_092409 (accessed January 7, 2013).

state, and local departments, led by two JTTFs [as] excellent and unprecedented."[29]

While the report offers conflicting assessments of the JTTF in the Hasan and Zazi cases, it illustrates concerns over JTTF consistency nationwide. On a comparable note, a 2009 Government Accountability Office report found that JTTFs were not effective for rural and tribal officials "because they did not have enough resources to dedicate personnel to the task forces."[30] Overall, the report questioned the reliance on informal information sharing by JTTFs with non-members in remote locations and those without appropriate security clearances, evidence of further room for improvement.

Aside from key examples noted previously, remarkably little public Congressional criticism exists with regards to JTTF performance, possibly a function of its marginal budget implications. Most recently available budget data for the JTTF dates to Fiscal Year (FY) 2004 and FY 2005, when its total budget was $286 million and $375 million, respectively.[31] During those years, personnel assigned to the task forces numbered 3,163 and 3,714, respectively.[32] Comparing those personnel numbers to the FY 2013 target of 4,590 task force members shows just under a 25% increase in personnel, roughly extrapolated into a parallel budget increase to $463 million for FY 2013. Considering the billions of dollars allocated to other homeland security spending, this paltry amount understandably avoids controversy or intense oversight from the Congress, another bonus for the JTTF model.

---

[29] Senate Committee on Homeland Security and Governmental Affairs, 55.

[30] U.S. Government Accountability Office (GAO), *Information Sharing: Federal Agencies are Sharing Border and Terrorism Information with Local and Tribal Law Enforcement Agencies, but Additional Efforts are Needed*, GAO (Washington, D.C., 2009), 24.

[31] U.S. Department of Justice, Office of the Inspector General, 15.

[32] U.S. Department of Justice, Federal Bureau of Investigation, *FY 2013 Authorization and Budget Request to Congress*, Federal Bureau of Investigation, (Washington, 2012), 44.

Executive Branch Appraisals of the JTTF

The Executive Branch has strongly endorsed the JTTF approach, but its support

has been low-key perhaps because scale the program exists in the shadow of the larger

FBI. Certainly, the White House relies on JTTF investigations to protect the homeland,

and a series of JTTF victories have made national headlines. Further support for the

concept is seen in remarks made by President Obama in 2009 to New York JTTF

members who he noted were "showing what focused and integrated counterterrorism

really looks like."[33] The Department of Justice's Office of the Inspector General (OIG)

completed an exhaustive review of JTTF operations in 2005. The report expressed

support for the JTTF as having "enhanced information sharing, partnerships, and

investigative capabilities for the Department's counterterrorism efforts" while also

strengthening "relationships with other federal, state, local, and private agencies."[34]

Similarly, the FBI website prominently features the JTTF achievements and argues that

all things counterterrorism feature a JTTF nexus.[35]

Despite breakneck growth and positive public relations, the Department of Justice

OIG found ample areas for improvement in JTTF management and operations in its 2005

report. First, the report challenges the lack of a national training plan for detailees

assigned to JTTFs, noting that some had received no counterterrorism since joining.[36]

Next, the report faults JTTFs for limited capacity to share information with partners in

remote areas outside of a JTTF's geographic location.[37] Though almost 8 years old, this

---

[33] The White House, "Remarks by the President to Joint Terrorism Task Force Staff Members," Office of the Press Secretary, http://www.whitehouse.gov/the-press-office/remarks-president-joint-terrorism-task-force-staff-members (accessed January 7, 2013).

[34] U.S. Department of Justice, Office of the Inspector General, x.

[35] Federal Bureau of Investigation, "Joint Terrorism Task Forces."

[36] U.S. Department of Justice, Office of the Inspector General, iv.

[37] Ibid., v.

criticism was repeated by the GAO in 2009, showing little progress made in this area and a weakness of the JTTF focus on major metropolitan areas and large population centers.[38] Additional shortcomings identified include staffing shortages, high turnover in leadership, and poor information technology connectivity, all of which are management issues that do not invalidate the JTTF model itself, but call for procedural changes.[39]

A final deficiency reported by the OIG stems from poor participation by the Drug Enforcement Administration and Immigration and Customs Enforcement, particularly the lack of manpower dedicated to JTTFs and inadequate direction from these agencies for its detailees.[40] These concerns weigh heavily on the ability of the JTTF to leverage a truly joint approach and illustrate underlying weaknesses in the personnel rotations of the task force model. Though JTTF membership is open to many partner agencies, opting out may hurt individual organizations as well as the larger effort. Bridging these types of gaps requires agreements at the Cabinet level coupled with firmer White House policy guidance. Examining JTTF perceptions and performance throughout its history provides critical lessons learned for not only improving the model, but also applying its strengths to the larger counterterrorism landscape. The JTTF struggles in three key areas that limit its effectiveness. The primary constraint on the JTTF model is its home inside the FBI system, acting at times as an independent piece of a sprawling organization with a reputation for inflexibility. Reliant on an FBI supervisor leading the team, guided by FBI procedures, and FBI culture, the JTTF's dynamism is threatened. A second challenge, influenced by and tied to the first, is investigative autonomy that facilitates competition. When individual field offices and their JTTFs succeed through investigative victories,

---

[38] U.S. Government Accountability Office, 24.
[39] Ibid.
[40] Ibid., ix.

culture and organization preclude sharing with competing offices or headquarters. A

final shortfall of the JTTF example is its limited scale despite a seemingly infinite scope.

Employing less than 5,000 members with an estimated budget under $1billion[41]

compared to the Department of Homeland Security's more than 200,000 personnel and a

FY 2012 enacted budget of $59.7 billion[42] shows how relatively small this effort is.

Despite these deficits, the model's positives certainly outweigh its negatives.

Three overarching JTTF strengths indicate the importance of the construct, its

ability to adapt, and argue for further refinement and expansion of the program. A trend

of inclusiveness and embracing local and other agency partners underpins the JTTF

model. With the understanding that partners augment their abilities, the FBI's effort to

have a standing forum with other players is central to creating a common

counterterrorism effort. Engaging local officials is a fine start towards creating a new

culture, but its full potential remains largely unrealized. An ideal adjustment would see a

JTTF managed not only by senior FBI agents in pursuit of FBI objectives, but with a

more diverse infrastructure. Endorsing such a change would mute criticism that the JTTF

is a cheap force multiplier for the FBI.

Next, the very autonomy that can hurt national efforts is a resource to be explored.

Tactics, techniques, and procedures tested at various JTTFs mean tailoring of resources to

a diverse country; consequently, best practices need to be captured by headquarters and

harnessed as a tool in the whole of nation counterterrorism effort. Finally, a central JTTF

strength is its very success and popularity. Leveraging its benefits, successes, and

flexibility is crucial for the FBI to reform its image in the eyes of other agencies and local

---

[41] U.S. Department of Justice, Federal Bureau of Investigation, *FY 2013 Authorization*, 44.
[42] U.S. Department of Homeland Security, *FY 2013 Budget in Brief*, Department of Homeland
Security, (Washington, 2013), 3.

officials. The task is made easier by embracing a widely-accepted model that is not perfect, but is able to adapt and grow.

Expanding the JTTF outside of major metropolitan areas is a natural tendency, but premature next step. More critical to maintaining counterterrorism gains is drawing the key themes from JTTF strengths and applying them to the widest audience possible. While this paper's thesis asserts that improved counterterrorism demands more equal partnerships, the temptation to apply one construct to a dynamic problem must be avoided. Creating JTTF Boone, Iowa may draw the support of residents and local leaders alike, but such a formula runs the risk of growth without critical thought, and ultimately detracts from national-level objectives. Following the example set in the previously-discussed HOA JTTF provide more equal partnerships where state and local officials help determine JTTF objectives. Recommendations to draw insight from this case study will examine these broad goals later in this paper.

CHAPTER 7: RECOMMENDATIONS

Creating unity of effort or an "all-of-Nation" approach is a lofty, yet critical objective to strengthening U.S. counterterrorism (CT) efforts. Protecting the United States as a whole requires some common ground between federal endeavors and those of the state and local partners who outnumber them and have a wider reach into communities. Three case studies on the New York City Police Department (NYPD), Department of Homeland Security (DHS), and Joint Terrorism Task Force (JTTF), reveal a divide between Washington and the periphery. These examples highlight root causes of diverging approaches in an attempt to turn challenges into opportunities. The following recommendations explore initial steps to reverse the trend of a U.S. counterterrorism policy that fails to consider and employ state and local partners. Ultimately, these recommendations support reforming counterterrorism practices before the next threat, responding to the severity of existing threats, eliminating institutional barriers, and better defining authorities.

NYPD Case Study

The NYPD Case Study highlights several deficiencies in U.S. counterterrorism policy. First, New York City's infusion of personnel and funding to counterterrorism efforts demonstrates a shortage of federal support in those areas. If federal counterterrorism efforts do not support state and local partners, let alone those at the highest risk, an adjustment in posture is required.

Recommendation #1

The NYPD Case Study portrays a city offering lessons to the federal government, underlining the weaknesses of a federal monopoly on counterterrorism. New York's experience demonstrates what true unity of effort can achieve as its transformation into a counterterrorism phenomenon stemmed from a mayor, police commissioner, city council, and public at-large with a common vision. The city's innovation and leap forward into CT expertise should encourage new formal links between state and local partners and the federal government. The State of Arizona's struggle to compel greater immigration enforcement represents another example of elevating a state issue to the national forefront, a strength of federalism that should be harnessed. The federal government should support state and local efforts to redraw counterterrorism boundaries, outsourcing some projects to willing and able partners to act as think tanks for problems that have national repercussions. A select group of highly capable actors – either major cities like Los Angeles or regional bodies – burden-sharing with the federal government presents the chance to develop local approaches to counterterrorism where federal resources are lacking.

Recommendation #2

A second recommendation derives from the NYPD's example of hiring former federal officials in order to create its own intelligence agency. The NYPD reaction is notable for what it does as much as what it addresses. The federal government still faces challenges sharing information with outside parties due in part to complicated regulations. The message from the NYPD's recruitment of federal officials, particularly those with intelligence backgrounds, is that there is no substitute for bringing together officials from all levels of government. Despite being retired or on a temporary detail to New York, the city leveraged the insider knowledge, contacts, and experience of these officials to improve New York's security, and by extension that of the entire nation.

To take advantage of state and local resources through professional exchanges, the United States must redouble efforts to enact provisions of the National Security Professional Development (NSPD) program initiated by the Bush Administration in 2007, which called for a "combination of shared education and training, and rotational tours of duty in other agencies, [so NSPs] would gain a better understanding of the mandates, capabilities, and cultures of other agencies[43] Weathering numerous changes since 2007, program guidance at one time had provisions for including state and local employees, but has since drifted in the face of challenges making it work on a federal level.[44] Recent history demonstrates that combining personnel from all levels of government is the foundation for achieving an "all-of-Nation" approach.

DHS Case Study

Roughly ten years of DHS employing massive grant programs and supporting the widespread growth of fusion centers without accomplishment illustrate a mismatch between DHS mission and capabilities. The poor performance of these critical programs is underscored by an absence of assessment tools to correct failures. Organizational challenges that prevent DHS from successfully administering its programs complicate its efforts to lead the "all-of-Nation" counterterrorism response. With responsibilities for

---

[1] Congressional Research Service, *National Security Professionals and Interagency Reform: Proposals, Recent Experience, and Issues for Congress, by Catherine Dale, Specialist in International Security, Congressional Research Service, September 26, 2011* (Washington, DC: Government Printing Office, 2011), 1.
[2] Ibid., 31.

federal counterterrorism efforts scattered across dozens of other agencies that operate independently of DHS, it cannot effectively coordinate U.S. counterterrorism.

Recommendation #3

The swelling DHS budget and struggle to define a viable mission demands close examination of DHS within the larger counterterrorism (CT) framework. Abolishing DHS is not the solution to the problem of a colossal and overtasked department, and would only undue recent strides to enhance its cohesion and narrow its mission. Since it is unlikely that DHS can emerge from a decade of inconsistencies as a true leader, it should move to a CT advisory role. Absent the unlikely designation of DHS as the Lead Federal Agency for CT, the United States should abandon further attempts to direct CT policy, instead assisting and advising state and local partners, through DHS.

Recommendation #4

The National Counterterrorism Center (NCTC) should be designated the Lead Federal Agency for CT, but only with an exhaustive guidelines for the responsibilities and authorities included with this title. The Federal Bureau of Investigation's (FBI) existing role as Lead Federal Agency should apply to CT investigations, but the FBI's organizational culture and deep history of autonomy does not position it well to coordinate across the U.S. government. Similarly, the National Security Council must retain overall coordination ability, but its design precludes it from true CT leadership. The NCTC's development, positive reception by the interagency community, and its ability to adapt to new threats makes it an ideal vehicle for greater responsibility, authority and leadership.

Recommendation #5

Congress should direct federal counterterrorism funds for state and local partners to an independent commission that allocates funds based on a transparent threat-based formula. In this example, a bipartisan group appointed by the President with the advice and consent of Congress would take the lead on disbursing counterterrorism funding, so that political considerations do not drive the process. Moving this process away from elected officials reduces the tendency for pork barrel spending outweighing threat-based spending.

Recommendation #6

The fusion center concept requires high-level attention and oversight in order to prevent duplication, waste, and risk creating a new bureaucracy. Similar to risk-based grants, if every state does not face the same threat, then not every state requires a fusion center. Consolidating some fusion centers into regional bodies offers greater efficiency and may reduce unnecessary redundancy. To this end, the Department of Homeland Security should conduct honest assessments of individual centers and close those that are not performing or useful. The larger fusion center concept faces greater risk from maintaining the status quo, or even growing further, than if its masters accept that its current footprint is both unsustainable and duplicative.

JTTF Case Study

The JTTF case study reveals a flexible model with many positive aspects, but remains limited in its scope and effectiveness. No two JTTFs operate the same, nor do they include representatives of the same agencies, a factor that can be leveraged to tailor

JTTF mission sets to geographic diversity. Widespread autonomy for JTTFs equates to a mixed blessing, sometimes stimulating innovation while also limiting contribution to national objectives. A small budget footprint, widespread support from local partners, and a record of successes establish the JTTF not as a counterterrorism panacea, but rather as an example of progress and a foundation for success.

Recommendation #7

The JTTF example should be strengthened in the short term, and expanded at a measured pace in the long term. With the ability to shape regional counterterrorism with influence disproportionate to meager budgets, the JTTF model demonstrates it is a powerful counterterrorism tool. In order to better leverage these autonomous tools, the FBI should do three things. First, the FBI should experiment with alternative management structure for JTTFs by launching a pilot program housed in a state or local law enforcement agency, and supervised by a representative from the same to avoid FBI dominance and increase incentives and responsibilities for partners. Next, the National JTTF should better coordinate, but not control, efforts across the numerous JTTFs to ensure that best practices are being shared and standardization exists without stunting innovation. Finally, though bringing the JTTF to every city is not the answer, additional geographic or even functional JTTFs should be created once the aforementioned recommendations are enacted. With functional JTTFs, a combination of law enforcement officials from all levels of government and geographic areas could combine to address specific threat areas such as homegrown radicals or international terrorists, as an answer to the seams created by existing geographic JTTFs.

CHAPTER 8: CONCLUSION

Separating the United States from the concept of counterterrorism in 2013 seems as unlikely as the events of September 11, 2001 to an observer one day earlier. Few aspects of American daily life are divorced from a counterterrorism that has been defined by roughly a decade of initiatives, first to strike back against a known enemy, and later to protect the country from new threats.

The attack of September 11, 2001 sparked a near-revolution in U.S. counterterrorism. Major government reorganization, expanding authorities for law enforce and intelligence organizations and a groundswell of public support set the conditions for massive reform to U.S. efforts to fight terrorism. The threat of terrorists striking U.S. soil has not diminished since 2001, and the absence of a major strike since then is evidence of improvements to the system.

Although the United States undoubtedly responded with intense efforts on many fronts to the growing threat of terrorism, these efforts have marginalized state and local partners, bedrocks of U.S. counterterrorism efforts. Existing outside the direct control of leaders in Washington, state and local partners vastly outnumber their federal counterparts and bring unparalleled expertise to protecting diverse communities in fifty states. As federal officials have kept state and local law enforcement on the periphery of U.S. counterterrorism reform, programs initiated by Washington have been adequate, but not sufficient to meet the long-term adapting threat.

In reviewing the existing U.S. counterterrorism landscape, this paper explored opportunities to improve national efforts through three case studies. Examining the cases of the New York City Police Department's creation of a shadow counterterrorism and intelligence system, the Department of Homeland Security's interaction with state and local partners through assistance programs and fusion centers, and the Federal Bureau of Investigation's Joint Terrorism Task Force shows cases ripe for improvement. As this paper's thesis statement posits, strengthening the domestic counterterrorism enterprise depends on Washington leading a more efficient system of interagency coordination and elevating the roles of state and local partners.

BIBLIOGRAPHY

Anonymous. "Homeland Security has $4 Billion in Police Grants for those who Learn Rules." *Crime Control Digest* 37, no. 25 (June 27, 2003): 1-2.

Associated Press. "AP's Probe into NYPD Intelligence Operations." Associated Press. http://www.ap.org/Index/AP-In-The-News/NYPD (accessed September 10, 2012).

Bornstein, Avram. "Antiterrorist Policing in New York City after 9/11: Comparing Perspectives on a Complex Process." *Human Organization* 64, no. 1(Spring 2005): 52-61.

Brzezinski, Matthew. *Fortress America: On the Front Lines of Homeland Security – An Inside Look at the Coming Surveillance State.* New York, NY: Bantam Books, 2004.

Byman, Daniel. *The Five Front War: The Better Way to Fight Global Jihad.* Hoboken, NJ: John Wiley & Sons, 2008.

City of New York. "Administration – Intelligence." New York City Police Department. http://www.nyc.gov/html/nypd/html/administration/intelligence_co.shtml (accessed October 29, 2012).

———. "Press Release: Remarks by Police Commissioner Kelly to Fordham Law Alumni, NYPD." http://www.nyc.gov/html/nypd/html/pr/pr_2012_03_03_remarks_to_fordham_law_school_alumni.shtml (accessed October 23, 2012).

———. "Mayor Michael R. Bloomberg And Police Commissioner Raymond W. Kelly Appoint United States Marine Lieutenant General Frank Libutti in Newly-Created Post of Deputy Commissioner of Counter-Terrorism." Office of the Mayor. http://www.nyc.gov/portal/site/nycgov/menuitem.b270a4a1d51bb3017bce0ed101c789a0/index.jsp?pageID=nyc_blue_room&catID=1194&doc_name=http%3A%2F%2Fwww.nyc.gov%2Fhtml%2Fom%2Fhtml%2F2002a%2Fpr012-02.html&cc=unused1978&rc=1194&ndi=1 (accessed October 29, 2012).

Coburn, Tom. *Safety At Any Price: Assessing the Impact of Homeland Security Spending in U.S. Cities.* Government Printing Office. Washington, DC, 2012.

Congressional Research Service. *Arizona v. United States: A Limited Role for States in Immigration Enforcement, by the Congressional Research Service, September 10, 2012.* Washington, DC: Government Printing Office, 2012.

———. *Department of Homeland Security Assistance to States and Localities: A Summary and Issues for the 111th Congress, by the Congressional Research Service, April 30, 2010.* Washington, DC: Government Printing Office, 2010.

———. *Department of Homeland Security Grants to State and Local Governments: FY2003 to FY 2006, by the Congressional Research Service, December 22, 2006.* Washington, DC: Government Printing Office, 2006.

———. *The Domestic Terrorist Threat: Background and Issues for Congress, by Jerome P. Bjelopera, Specialist in Organized Crime and Terrorism, Congressional Research Service, May 15, 2012.* Washington, DC: Government Printing Office, 2012.

———. *The Federal Bureau of Investigation and Terrorism Investigations, by the Congressional Research Service, December 28, 2011.* Washington, DC: Government Printing Office, 2011.

———. *Fusion Centers: Issues and Options for Congress, by John Rollins, Congressional Research Service, January 18, 2008.* Washington, DC: Government Printing Office, 2008.

———. *Intelligence and Law Enforcement: Countering Transnational Threats to the U.S., by Richard A. Best, Jr., Specialist in National Defense, Congressional Research Service, December 3, 2001.* Washington, DC: Government Printing Office, 2001.

———. *The National Counterterrorism Center (NCTC) – Responsibilities and Potential Congressional Concerns, by Richard A. Best, Specialist in National Defense, Congressional Research Service, December 19, 2011.* Washington, DC: Government Printing Office, 2011.

———. *The National Security Council: An Organizational Assessment, by Richard A. Best, Jr., Specialist in National Defense, Congressional Research Service, December 28, 2011.* Washington, DC: Government Printing Office, 2011.

———. *National Security Professionals and Interagency Reform: Proposals, Recent Experience, and Issues for Congress, by Catherine Dale, Specialist in International Security, Congressional Research Service, September 26, 2011.* Washington, DC: Government Printing Office, 2011.

———. *Presidential Directives: Background and Overview, by Harold C. Relyea, Specialist in American National Government, Congressional Research Service, February 10, 2003.* Washington, DC: Government Printing Office, 2003.

Deflem, Mathieu. "Joint Terrorism Task Forces." In *Counterterrorism: From the Cold War to the War on Terror, Volume 1*, 423-426. Santa Barbara, CA: Praeger, 2012.

Dickey, Christopher. *Securing The City: Inside America's Best Counterterror Force – The NYPD*. New York, NY: Simon & Schuster, 2009.

Donley, Michael, Cornelius O'Leary, and John Montgomery. "Inside the White House Situation Room: A National Nerve Center." Central Intelligence Agency Center for the Study of Intelligence. https://www.cia.gov/library/center-for-the-study-of-intelligence/csi-publications/csi-studies/studies/97unclass/whithous.html (accessed January 10, 2013).

Eisinger, Peter. "Imperfect Federalism: The Intergovernmental Partnership for Homeland Security." *Public Administration Review* 66, no. 4 (July/August 2006): 537-545.

Erickson, Kris, John Carr, and Steve Herbert. "The Scales of Justice: Federal-Local Tensions in the War on Terror," in *Uniform Behavior: Police Localism and National Politics*, 231-253 . Gordonsville, VA: Palgrave Macmillan, 2006.

Federal Bureau of Investigation. "Joint Terrorism Task Forces." Federal Bureau of Investigation. http://www.fbi.gov/about-us/investigate/terrorism/terrorism_jttfs (accessed December 14, 2012).

———. "New York Terror Case: Indictment Announced." Federal Bureau of Investigation. http://www.fbi.gov/news/stories/2009/september/zazi_092409 (accessed January 7, 2013).

Fleming, Sibley. "Where Did the Buck Stop?" *American City & County* 118, no. 8 (July 2004): 41-46.

General Accounting Office. *Combating Terrorism: Issues to Be Resolved to Improve Counterterrorism Operations, by the General Accounting Office*. Washington, DC: Government Printing Office, 1999.

———. *Combating Terrorism: Linking Threats to Strategies and Resources, by Norman J. Rabkin, Director National Security Preparedness Issues, General Accounting Office*. Washington, DC: Government Printing Office, 2000.

Government Accountability Office. *Homeland Security: Management of First Responder Grant Programs and Efforts to Improve Accountability Continue to Evolve, by William O. Jenkins, Jr., Director Homeland Security and Justice Issues, Government Accountability Office*. Washington, DC: Government Printing Office, 2005.

———. *Information Sharing: Federal Agencies are Sharing Border and Terrorism Information with Local and Tribal Law Enforcement Agencies, but Additional Efforts are Needed, by the Government Accountability Office*. Washington, DC: Government Printing Office, 2009.

House Committee on Homeland Security. Subcommittee on Emergency Preparedness, Response, and Communication. *Homeland Security Grants Oversight: Testimony of Richard Daddario.* Government Printing Office. Washington, DC, 2012.

Jeffreys-Jones, Rhodri. *The FBI: A History.* New Haven, CT: Yale University Press, 2007.

Johnson, Loch K. "Congressional Supervision of America's Secret Agencies: The Experience and Legacy of the Church Committee." *Public Administration Review* 64, no. 1 (January/February 2004): 3-14.

Kayyem, Juliette. "Never Say 'Never Again'." Foreign Policy. http://www.foreignpolicy.com/articles/2012/09/10/never_say_never_again?print=yes&hidecomments=yes&page=full (accessed October 26, 2012).

Kettl, Donald F. "The Deparment of Homeland Security's First Year." The Century Foundation. http://tcf.org/publications/2004/3/pb451 (accessed November 28, 2012).

———. "Unconnected Dots." *Governing* 17, no. 7 (April 2004): 14-14.

Lakoff, Andrew and Eric Klinenberg. "Of Risk and Pork: Urban Security and the Politics of Objectivity." *Theory and Society* 39, no. 5 (September 2010): 509-525.

Lipowicz, Alice. "A Guide to Where the Grants Are." Special Issue. *Governing* Securing the Homeland (October 2004): 37-44.

Martin, Robert A. "The Joint Terrorism Task Force: A Concept that Works." *FBI Law Enforcement Bulletin* 68, no. 3 (March 1999): 23-27.

Mayer, Matt A. "Pork Payoffs in Homeland Security Jeopardize Americans." The Heritage Foundation. http://www.heritage.org/research/commentary/2010/01/pork-payoffs-in-homeland-security-jeopardize-americans (accessed February 12, 2013).

Monahan, Torin. "The Future of Security? Surveillance Operations at Homeland Security Fusion Centers." *Social Justice* 37, no. 2-3 (2010-2011): 84-98.

Monahan, Torin and Neal A. Palmer. "The Emerging Politics of DHS Fusion Centers." *Security Dialogue* 40, no. 6 (December 2009): 617-636.

National Commission on Terrorist Attacks Upon the United States. *Final Report of the National Commission on Terrorist Attacks Upon the United States.* Government Printing Office. Washington, DC, 2004.

National Counterterrorism Center. "About the National Counterterrorism Center." National Counterterrorism Center. http://www.nctc.gov/about_us/about_nctc.html (accessed August 17, 2012).

The National Security Archive. "From Director of Central Intelligence to Director of National Intelligence." George Washington University. http://www.gwu.edu/~nsarchiv/NSAEBB/NSAEBB144/index.htm (accessed January 14, 2013).

Nussbaum, Brian. "From Brescia to Bin Laden: The NYPD, International Policing, and 'National Security'." *Journal of Applied Security Research* 7, no. 2 (April 2012): 178-202.

———. "Protecting Global Cities: New York, London, and the Internationalization of Municipal Policing for Counter Terrorism." *Global Crime* 8, no. 3 (August 2007): 213-232.

Partnership for Public Service. "The Best Places to Work in the Federal Government." Partnership for Public Service. http://www.bestplacestowork.org/BPTW/rankings/detail/HS00 (accessed December 12, 2012).

Rittgers, David. "Abolish the Department of Homeland Security." The Cato Institute. http://www.cato.org/publications/policy-analysis/abolish-department-homeland-security (accessed September 10 2012).

Rozen, Laura. "Introducing the National Security Staff." Politico. http://www.politico.com/blogs/laurarozen/0110/Introducing_the_National_Security_Staff.html (accessed January 10, 2013).

Rudman, Warren. *Emergency Responders: Drastically Underfunded, Dangerously Unprepared: Report of an Independent Task Force Sponsored by the Council on Foreign Relations.* New York, NY: Council on Foreign Relations Press, 2003.

Senate Committee on Homeland Security and Governmental Affairs. *A Ticking Time Bomb: Counterterrorism Lessons from the U.S. Government's Failure to Prevent the Fort Hood Attack.* Government Printing Office. Washington, DC, 2011.

———. Senate Permanent Subcommittee on Investigations. *Federal Support for and Inolvement in State and Local Fusion Centers.* Majority and Minority Staff report. Government Printing Office. Washington, DC, 2012.

Smith, Brent L. *Terrorism in America: Pipe Bombs and Pipe Dreams.* Albany, NY: State University of New York Press, 1994.

Stewart, Scott. "Growing Concern Over the NYPD's Counterterrorism Methods." Stratfor Global Intelligence. http://www.stratfor.com/weekly/20111012-growing-concern-over-nypds-counterterrorism-methods (accessed October 26, 2012).

Thacher, David. "The Local Role in Homeland Security." *Law & Society Review* 39, no. 3 (September 2005): 635-676.

U.S. Department of Homeland Security. *Brief Documentary History of the Department of Homeland* Security, History Office. Government Printing Office. Washington, DC, 2008.

———. *The Federal Emergency Management Agency's Requirements for Reporting Homeland Security Grant Program Achievements*. Office of the Inspector General. Government Printing Office. Washington, DC, 2012.

———. "Fusion Center Success Stories," U.S. Department of Homeland Security. http://www.dhs.gov/fusion-center-success-stories (accessed December 13, 2012).

———. *FY 2013 Budget in Brief*. Department of Homeland Security, Government Printing Office. Washington, DC, 2013.

———. *Keynote Address by Secretary of Homeland Security Michael Chertoff to the 2006 Grants & Training National Conference*, by Michael Chertoff, Secretary of Homeland Security. Government Printing Office. Washington, D.C., 2006.

———. "National Network of Fusion Center Fact Sheet." U.S. Department of Homeland Security. http://www.dhs.gov/national-network-fusion-centers-fact-sheet (accessed December 13, 2012).

———. *Quadrennial Homeland Security Review Report: A Strategic Framework for a Secure Homeland*. Government Printing Office. Washington, DC, 2010.

U.S. Department of Justice, Community Oriented Policing Services "Protecting Your Community from Terrorism: Strategies for Local Law Enforcement, Volume 1: Local-Federal Partnerships," Police Executive Research Forum. Washington, DC, 2003.

———. Bureau of Justice Assistance. *Fusion Center Guidelines: Developing and Sharing Information and Intelligence in a New Era*. Office of Justice Programs. Government Printing Office. Washington, DC, 2006.

———. Federal Bureau of Investigation. *FY 2013 Authorization and Budget Request to Congress*. Federal Bureau of Investigation. Government Printing Office. Washington, DC, 2012.

———. Federal Bureau of Investigation. *Terrorism in the United States – 1993*, Terrorist Research and Analytical Center, National Security Division (Washington, DC: Government Printing Office, 1994), 26.

———. Office of the Inspector General. *The Department of Justice's Terrorism Task Forces*. Evaluation and Inspections Division. Government Printing Office. Washington, DC, 2005.

U.S. Joint Chiefs of Staff, *Counterterrorism*, Joint Publication 3-26 (Washington DC: Joint Chiefs of Staff, November 13, 2009).

———. *Joint Tactics, Techniques, and Procedures for Antiterrorism*. Joint Publication 3-07.2. Washington DC: Joint Chiefs of Staff, March 17, 1998.

U.S. National Commission on Terrorism. Countering the Changing Threat of International Terrorism: Report of the National Commission on Terrorism (Washington, DC: Government Printing Office, August 2000).

U.S. President. *National Security Strategy.* Washington DC: Government Printing Office, May 2010.

———. *National Strategy for Homeland Security.* Washington DC: Government Printing Office, July 2002.

———. *National Strategy for Homeland Security.* Washington, DC: Government Printing Office, October 2007.

—— *Presidential Decision Directive 39: U.S. Policy on Counterterrorism.* Washington DC: Government Printing Office, June 21, 1995.

—— *Presidential Policy Directive 8: National Preparedness.* Washington DC: Government Printing Office, March 30, 2011.

The Washington Institute. "Defending the City: NYPD's Counterterrorism Operations." Policy Watch. http://www.washingtoninstitute.org/policy-analysis/view/defending-the-city-nypds-counterterrorism-operations (accessed October 26, 2012).

Waxman, Matthew C. "National Security Federalism in the Age of Terror." *Stanford Law Review* 64, no. 289 (February 2012): 289-350.

The White House. "Remarks by the President to Joint Terrorism Task Force Staff Members." Office of the Press Secretary. http://www.whitehouse.gov/the-press-office/remarks-president-joint-terrorism-task-force-staff-members (accessed January 7, 2013).

White, Mary Jo. "Prosecuting Terrorism in New York." *Middle East Quarterly* 8, no. 2 (Spring 2001):11-18.

Wise, Charles R. and Rania Nader. "Organizing the Federal System for Homeland Security: Problems, Issues, and Dilemmas." Special Issue. *Public Administration Review* 62 (September 2002): 44-57.

VITA

Ryan Hawkins joined the Department of State in 2006 as a Special Agent with the Diplomatic Security Service (DSS). His prior assignments have included: Assistant Regional Security Officer, U.S. Embassy Jakarta, Indonesia; Assistant Shift Leader, Secretary of State Protective Detail; U.S. Ambassador to the United Nations Protective Detail; and the New York Field Office. Mr. Hawkins has a Bachelor's Degree in Government and Spanish from Manhattan College.